AN UNOFFICIAL ENCYCLOPEDIA OF STRATEGY FOR FORTNITERS

BATTLE ROYALE FOR NOOBS

AN UNOFFICIAL ENCYCLOPEDIA OF STRATEGY FOR FORTNITERS

BATTLE ROYALE FOR NOOBS

JASON R. RICH

Sky Pony Press
New York

10 9 8 7 6 5 4 3 2 1

Library of Congress Cataloging-in-Publication Data is available on file.

Series design by Brian Peterson

Hardcover ISBN: 978-1-5107-4457-8
E-book ISBN: 978-1-5107-4465-3

Printed in China

TABLE OF CONTENTS

AN UNOFFICIAL ENCYCLOPEDIA OF STRATEGY FOR FORTNITERS

BATTLE ROYALE FOR NOOBS

SECTION 1

OVERVIEW OF *FORTNITE: BATTLE ROYALE*

You're about to embark on a combat-oriented adventure unlike any other. It's an experience that'll put your exploration, building, combat, and survival skills to the ultimate test. You'll shortly find yourself controlling a soldier who is transported to a mysterious island for each match you participate in.

Keep in mind, even if you know everything there is to know about this game (there's a lot to learn), to become a truly awesome player is going to take practice . . . a lot of practice! Don't get discouraged if you're not immediately able to defeat your enemies, or consistently achieve #1 Victory Royale.

For about 15 minutes per match, you'll face dangerous enemies, contend with a deadly storm, and do whatever it takes to ultimately achieve one thing—#1 Victory Royale. This means you emerge as the last person alive on the island at the end of a match. Everyone else must perish, resulting in their immediate elimination.

The Ultimate Fortnite: Battle Royale Encyclopedia for Noobs is specifically for gamers who have never experienced the mega-popular game *Fortnite: Battle Royale* from Epic Games. A noob is a beginner, and this guide is written specifically for beginners.

Whether you're experiencing this game on a PC, Mac, PlayStation 4, Xbox One, Nintendo Switch, Apple iPhone, Apple iPad, or an Android-based mobile device, this unofficial guide will teach you exactly what you need to know, so you can get started playing *Fortnite: Battle Royale and* understand what's going on.

One of the things that will help you become a better player is your ability to aim and shoot the many different types of weapons your soldier will encounter on the island.

You also need to work on your building skills, understand the layout of the island (and how to read the island map), and discover how and when to avoid the deadly storm.

Plus, you definitely want to get acquainted with the many loot items your soldier can collect and use throughout each match to help him or her survive longer. All of this will be explained within this unofficial guide. You'll also discover hundreds of proven tips and strategies that over time can make you a better *Fortnite: Battle Royale* gamer.

Welcome to the Mysterious Island

Each time you launch *Fortnite: Battle Royale* on your gaming system, the soldier you'll be controlling is displayed in the center of the Lobby screen. Once you customize the appearance of your soldier from the Locker, and if you choose, tweak any of the game's settings, you will select which game play mode you want to experience.

Fortnite: Battle Royale offers three permanent game play modes: **Solo, Duos, and Squads.** These are always available. In addition, you'll often discover temporary game play modes that are available for short periods of time. Some of these include Playground, or some type of 50 v 50 game.

What You Should Know About Game Play Modes

A **Solo** game allows you to control one soldier, who competes against up to 99 other soldiers (each controlled by a different player in real time). At the end of a match, only one soldier will remain standing. This is *Fortnite: Battle Royale*'s most popular game play mode.

When you play a **Duos** game, you and a partner (either an online friend or a stranger) get to team up and work together in order to defeat up to 98 other soldiers who are placed on the island at the same time as you. The goal is for you *and* your partner to survive and be the last two soldiers alive at the end of each match.

By choosing the **Squads** game play mode, you and up to three online friends (or strangers) team up to form a four-person squad. You'll then work together as you compete against up to 96 other gamers, each of whom is also part of a four-person squad.

Playground mode allows you alone (or a group of online friends or strangers) to get transported to the island for about 55 minutes, during which time you can explore, build, and participate in practice battles, without worrying about getting defeated by enemies or perishing within the storm. When the Playground mode is available, it provides the perfect place to practice your fighting, building, exploration, and survival skills.

When a 50 v 50 match is offered, 100 gamers are divided into two teams. The goal is for one team to defeat the other. This game play mode allows you to participate in massive firefights (with your teammates) against often large groups of enemy soldiers.

Discover What Happens During a Match

Each match in *Fortnite: Battle Royale* lasts about 15 minutes. After choosing a game play mode from the Choose Game Mode menu screen, you'll be returned back to the Lobby. The Choose Game Mode screen displays each available gaming mode, including Solo, Duos, Squads, and whichever other game play modes are currently available.

Select the Play option from the Lobby, and your soldier will be transported to the

pre-deployment area. It's here you'll wait for up to 99 other gamers to join the match. Once this happens, everyone boards the flying Battle Bus.

The blue Battle Bus then flies over the island where each match takes place. It doesn't land, however. You must decide when you want your soldier to leap from the bus and freefall toward land.

Either while you're in the pre-deployment area, or once you're aboard the Battle Bus, view the island map and select your desired landing destination, based on the random route the Battle Bus takes as it travels over the island.

As your soldier is freefalling from the Battle Bus toward land, use the directional arrows on your controller (or keyboard/mouse) to navigate toward your desired landing location. To make your soldier fall faster, point him or her in a downward direction. You'll discover that landing quickly and beating enemy soldiers to your landing location will always work to your advantage.

Once your soldier lands, he or she is armed only with their pickaxe and an empty backpack. Your first task should be to find and grab a weapon and ammo, so you can protect yourself. You'll also want to find cover, so you don't immediately get attacked by enemy soldiers until you've built up your arsenal and you're ready to engage in battle. However, as you'll discover, this is not always an option.

Before your soldier crashes on land with a splat, his or her glider activates. This slows down your soldier's rate of descent and gives you more precise navigational control. You can activate or deactivate the glider at any time during the freefall.

Your soldier's pickaxe can be used as a rather weak, short-range weapon. It'll take multiple direct hits to defeat an enemy. It's also used to smash objects and harvest resources (wood, stone, and metal), as well as to destroy obstacles and objects in your path that need to be removed.

Almost everything on the island can be smashed with a pickaxe. Depending on what you're smashing is made out of, you'll wind up harvesting wood, stone, or metal. These are the resources you'll use for building. Resources can also be used with a Vending Machine to purchase powerful weapons and loot items, but more on that later.

Beware of the Deadly Storm!

Minutes after you land on the island at the start of a match, a deadly storm forms and begins to expand and move. All soldiers need to avoid the storm. For every second a soldier gets caught in the storm, his or her Health meter diminishes. The damage the storm causes per second intensifies as a match progresses, so ideally, you should avoid the storm altogether. This is not always possible, however.

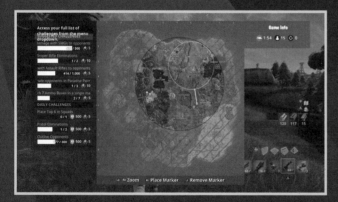

As the storm expands, all surviving soldiers are forced to move closer and closer together, as the amount of habitable land on the island shrinks.

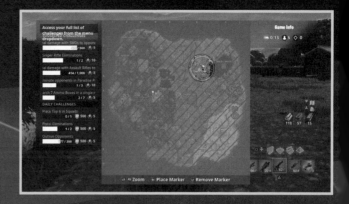

Near the end of a match, only a few soldiers will remain alive and they'll be confined to a very tiny circle of inhabitable land on the island. This is called the Final Circle or the End Game. It's when and where the final battles take place until only one soldier (or one team) remains alive.

Pay Attention to Your Soldier's Health and Shield Meters

A green bar is displayed at the bottom-center of the screen (on most gaming systems). This represents your soldier's Health meter. At the start of a match, your soldier's Health meter is maxed out at 100. Each time he or she gets injured (as a result of a fight, a fall, or the storm, for example), some of their health gets depleted.

When a soldier's Health meter reaches zero, he or she is immediately eliminated from the

By consuming or using powerup loot items, like a Chug Jug, Med Kit, or Bandages, for example, you can boost your soldier's Health meter. Each of these powerups works slightly differently and takes a different amount of time to consume or use, during which time your soldier is vulnerable to attack.

Displayed directly above a soldier's Health meter is a blue bar that represents their Shield meter. At the start of a match, the Shield meter is at zero. To activate and boost your soldier's shields, consume or use a powerup loot item, such as Mushrooms (shown here), a Small Shield Potion, or a Shield Potion.

The Shield meter also maxes out at 100. Shields will protect your soldier from weapon attacks and explosions, but not from the storm or falls. Before going into a battle, try to ensure both your Health and Shield meters

Be Ready to Juggle Many Responsibilities, Not Just Fight!

Once you've landed on the island, you'll need to handle many responsibilities at once, related to exploration, fighting, building, and survival. Be prepared to:

1. Safely explore the island.
2. Avoid the deadly storm. Spending time in the storm causes damage to your soldier's health, so this is not someplace you want to get caught.
3. Harvest and collect resources, including wood, stone, and metal.
4. Locate, collect, and manage your personal arsenal of weapons. Knowing that you'll soon be facing many enemies, think about if you will need to engage in close-range combat, mid-range combat, or long-range combat, and build up your arsenal accordingly. This is typically determined, in part, by the terrain you're currently in. As you move around, the terrain changes, as will your arsenal requirements.
5. Find and collect plenty of ammunition for the types of weapons you'll be using. There are five types of ammunition; each works with different types of weapons. A weapon that runs out of ammunition is worthless.
6. Acquire and properly use loot items that can help you survive.
7. Manage the inventory in your soldier's backpack (which only has six slots capable of holding weapons and/or loot items, including your soldier's pickaxe).
8. Build ramps, bridges, structures, and fortresses using collected resources in

locations, or to provide defensive shielding during attacks.

9. Engage in combat and firefights with enemy soldiers.

10. Gather what you'll need for the End Game as you enter into the Final Circle.

If you'll be participating in a Duos, Squads, or 50 v 50 match, you'll have three additional responsibilities, which include:

- Reviving your partner or squad members who get injured before their Health meter gets fully depleted and they're eliminated from the match. Remember, you're rewarded for helping others, just as you're rewarded for defeating enemies.
- Sharing weapons, ammo, loot items, and resources, as needed, with your teammates.
- Communicating with your partner, squad members, or teammates to coordinate well-timed and expertly planned attacks, while working together to defend yourselves.

Every Match You Experience Will Be Different

Because all your enemies in *Fortnite: Battle Royale* are controlled by other gamers in real time, you never know how someone will react in a particular situation, so you must be able to adapt your offensive or defensive strategies, based on the actions of your enemies.

The island where matches takes place is comprised of more than 20 different locations that are labeled on the island map, along with many smaller locations that aren't labeled. Depending on the landing site you choose

and the random path the deadly storm follows as it moves and expands, you'll be forced to explore and fight within many different types of terrain.

To keep the game interesting and very difficult to master, every week or two, Epic Games releases a game update (called a patch). With each new update, several things might change, including:

- New weapons are added to the game, or the capabilities of existing weapons are tweaked (changed). When a weapon or item's strength or capabilities are made weaker by Epic Games, this is referred to as being "nerfed."
- New (unlabeled) points of interest (locations) are added to the island, giving you more places to explore.
- New loot items are added to the game, while others are "vaulted," or their capabilities are adjusted. (When something is "vaulted," it is removed from the game by Epic Games but could be reintroduced into the game at any time in the future.)
- The defensive Hit Point (HP) strength of building tiles (used to build structures, ramps, and fortresses) or other items within the game are modified.
- New ways to travel around and explore the island are added or removed from the game. While your soldier can always walk, run, crouch, jump, or tiptoe, for example, items that can be used to help transport your soldier around— like All Terrain Karts, Shopping Carts, Grapplers, Launch Pads, Bouncer Pads, Rifts, and Jet Packs—are constantly being added or removed from the game by Epic Games.

In addition to regular game patches, major game updates are introduced every two to three months, in conjunction with each new game season. At the start of a new season, you can expect major changes to be made to various points of interest (locations) on the island. Some will be replaced, while new locations are introduced. You can also expect other major game play changes to be implemented.

Each time something new is added to *Fortnite: Battle Royale*, a News window is displayed when you launch the game. For more details about new additions and changes to the game, visit: www.epicgames.com/fortnite/en-US/news.

What You Can Learn from the Island Map and Location Map

Any time you're in the pre-deployment area, on the Battle Bus, or on the island itself, you have access to the island map. There are several versions of the island map you need to become acquainted with.

Continuously displayed on the screen during a match is the Location Map. It shows a small area of the island around your current location. Your exact location is displayed as a white triangle. The location of your partner, squad mates, or teammates are displayed as colored triangles. This map's location on the screen will vary depending on which gaming platform you're using. It's shown here on a PS4, in the top-right corner of the screen. Unfortunately, you can't ever see the location of your enemies on any map.

If you see a white line linked with your location icon (the white triangle) on the Location Map (shown) or island map, this is the path to follow to reach the safe area of the island to avoid the storm's movement and expansion.

During the time you're in the pre-deployment area waiting to board the Battle Bus, or for the first 20 seconds or so that you're riding the bus, access the large island map to see the random route the Battle Bus will be taking over the island. Knowing this can help you choose a landing location.

Checking the island map during a match reveals a lot of useful information.

Here's what you can see on the island map during a match:

- The random route the Battle Bus will take across the island. This route is only displayed while you're in the pre-deployment area and for the first few seconds while aboard the Battle Bus.
- The location of each point of interest on the island. The major points of interest are labeled. Many of the smaller points

of interest, located between the major points of interest, are not labeled.
- Your current location.
- The location of your partner, squad mates, or team members, depending on which game play mode you're experiencing.
- The current location of the storm. The storm-ravaged areas are always displayed in pink.
- The area of the island that's currently inhabitable is displayed inside the large circle on the map.
- Where the safe area (inhabitable land) on the island will be after the storm moves and expands next is displayed within the inner circle you'll often see on the island map.
- If markers have been placed on the map, these too are displayed. Markers are used to select a rendezvous location or desired landing location. Markers can be displayed on the island map for only you and your allies (not your enemies) to see.

Once you set markers on the island map, colored flares also appear on the main game screen. Use a marker/flare to set a meetup location anytime during a match.

Check the timer (displayed directly below the Location Map) frequently to determine when the storm will be expanding and moving next, and make sure you're able to avoid the storm as much as possible.

Remember, the storm moves faster than your soldier can run, so unless you have an All Terrain Kart, Shopping Cart, Bouncer Pads, Launch Pads, Jetpack, or Rift-to-Go, don't plan on trying to outrun the storm if you'll need to cover a long distance.

Learn How Map Coordinates Work

Whenever you look at the large island map, you'll discover it's divided into quadrants. Along the top of the map are the letters "A" through "J." Along the left edge of the map are the numbers "1" through "10." Each point of interest or location on the map can be found by its unique coordinates.

For example, Tilted Towers is found at map coordinates D5.5, and Snobby Shores is located at coordinates A5. At the start of Season 5, Paradise Palms replaced Moisty Mire and was centered around map coordinates I8, while Anarchy Acres was replaced by Lazy Links at map coordinates F2.5. The unlabeled Viking village (which contains the Viking ship) can be found on a mountaintop near map coordinates B4.5.

Building Is an Essential Skill in *Fortnite: Battle Royale*

Becoming an expert builder, especially in the heat of battle, requires practice, as well as some creativity when it comes to designing structures. Either by watching livestreams of

expert players on YouTube or Twitch.tv, or by staying in Spectator mode once you're eliminated from a match, watch the final stages of matches carefully to learn the best techniques for building fortresses.

When you're learning to build in *Fortnite: Battle Royale*, experiment with different structure designs, and develop the skillset needed to be able to build very quickly, without having to think too much about it. If the Playground game play mode is currently offered (it's added and removed from the game periodically), this is the perfect place to practice your building techniques. Some of the screenshots you'll see throughout this unofficial guide were captured while using the Playground game play mode on a PS4.

Switching Between Combat Mode and Building Mode

During a match, your soldier can either be in Combat mode or Building mode. In other words, he or she can be holding and using a weapon or building—both can't be done at the same time. Be sure to practice switching between Combat mode and Building mode, so you can do this quickly.

Also, when your soldier is using a powerup loot item, he or she will not be able to do anything else during that time. It's important that before you use one of these items, you position your soldier in a safe place.

Each Building Tile Has Its Own Strength

There are four shapes of building tiles—vertical wall tiles, horizontal floor/ceiling tiles, ramp/stair tiles, and pyramid-shaped tiles. Once you enter into Building mode, first choose your building material. Next, decide where you want to build. Finally, one at a time, select which building tile you want to use.

Each tile has an HP level, which determines how much damage it can withstand before collapsing or being destroyed. During the building process, a tile's HP increases gradually. Wood is the fastest to build with, while working with stone is slightly slower. Metal takes the longest to build with but ultimately offers the most protection.

Each tile costs 10 of the selected resource to build. Remember, when you're in Building mode, you can't use a weapon. You'll definitely need to practice quickly switching between Combat mode and Building mode.

When you go into Edit mode to alter a tile—to add a door or window, for example—the defensive strength (HP) of that tile changes. Each tile has its own HP meter which is displayed when your soldier faces the tile.

The trick to becoming a highly skilled builder is speed. Achieving speed takes practice! Here are some additional strategies to help you become an expert builder. In order to build in *Fortnite: Battle Royale*, you must first collect or harvest resources (wood, stone, and metal).

The resource icons you discover lying on the ground, within chests, within Loot Llamas, and within Supply Drops, allow you to quickly grab bundles of specific resources. You can also pick up resources discarded by a defeated enemy when they're eliminated from the match.

First Harvest or Collect Resources and Then Build

Large and thick trees can be seen from a distance. When smashing a tree with your pickaxe to harvest wood, if you fully destroy the tree, it crashes to the ground and disappears. This is something that nearby enemies will notice, and it will give away your location. To avoid this, as you're smashing a tree, keep an eye on

its HP meter. As soon as it starts to get low, stop smashing that tree (while it's still standing) and move on. You'll still collect wood, but the tree will remain standing. To harvest more wood, simply walk to another tree and repeat the process.

Smashing anything made out of wood that you encounter on the island allows you to harvest wood. Trees and wooden pallets tend to generate a lot of wood. Smashing the walls, floor, or roof of most structures also generates wood, unless the structure is made from a different material.

Smashing anything made of brick or stone generates stone.

Smashing anything made of metal, such as appliances within a home, machinery within a factory or building, or any type of vehicle (in this case an RV) will generate metal.

What You Should Know About Weapons, Ammo, and Loot Items

There are many different types of weapons available on the island that your soldier can find, grab, and then utilize in a firefight or any combat situation. The different types of guns shoot bullets (or shells). For them to function, in addition to gathering guns within your arsenal, you'll also need to gather and collect ammunition that works with the weapons you have.

Other types of guns, like shotguns, are better suited for close-to-mid-range combat.

Different types of rifles, are ideal for long-range combat.

Some guns, like various types of pistols, are ideal for close-range combat.

It's also possible to add explosive weapons, like Grenades, Remote Explosives, Clingers, Boogie Bombs, Stick Bombs, and Impulse Grenades to your soldier's arsenal. Most of these cause explosions and are tossed at a target by your solder. They're best suited as mid-range weapons. If your soldier is too close to an explosion, he too will get injured.

In addition, there are long-range, projectile weapons that cause explosions and are very powerful. Rocket Launchers, Guided Missile Launchers, and Grenade Launchers, for example, can be used to defeat enemies from a distance, and can quickly destroy structures.

As you'll discover, all weapons are categorized in several different ways, including by their rarity (which also determines how powerful they are).

Weapons with a **green** hue are "Uncommon."

Weapons with a **blue** hue are "Rare."

Weapons with a **grey** hue are "Common."

Weapons with a **purple** hue are "Epic."

Gameskinny.com (www.gameskinny.com/9mt22 /complete-fortnite-battle-royale-weapons- stats-list), and RankedBoost.com (https:// rankedboost.com/fortnite/best-weapons-tier -list), that provide the current stats for each weapon offered in *Fortnite: Battle Royale*, based on the latest tweaks made to the game. Just make sure when you look at this information online, it refers to the most recently released version of *Fortnite: Battle Royale*.

Weapons with an **orange** hue are "Legendary." They tend to be harder to find, extra powerful, and very rare. If you're able to obtain one, grab it! When experiencing a 50 v 50 match, you're most apt to find "Legendary" weapons within Supply Drops or by defeating enemies. They do periodically show up elsewhere, however.

It is possible to collect several of the same weapon, but each could have a different rarity. So, if you collect two of the same weapon type and one is rare, but the second is legendary, definitely keep the legendary weapon and trade the other for something else when you find a replacement.

How to Learn About the Power of Weapons and the Damage Each Can Cause

If you're really interested in how a weapon is rated, evaluate its DPR (Damage Per Second) rating, overall Damage Rating, Fire Rate, MAG (Magazine) Capacity, and Reload Time. This is information that Epic Games tweaks often. Select a weapon you're carrying and then view your Backpack Inventory screen to see details about it.

There are plenty of websites, including: IGN.

Choose Your Arsenal Wisely

Based on where you are, what challenges you're currently facing, the distance you are from your target(s), and what you anticipate your needs will be, stock your backpack with the weapons and tools you think you'll need for the battles and challenges ahead.

The various types of ammunition you've collected, how much of each ammo type you have on hand, and which weapons each ammo type can be used with, is also displayed on the Backpack Inventory screen. While viewing this screen, select a specific ammunition type to learn more about it. Here you can see that Medium Bullets has been selected from the Backpack Inventory screen. This soldier has 162 of these mid-range caliber bullets on hand. This type of ammo is used with assault

How and Where to Collect Ammo

Without having the appropriate ammunition on hand, whatever weapons you're carrying will be useless. Throughout each match, there are several ways to find and collect ammo.

- Ammunition can be collected from ammo boxes. These are scattered throughout the island, and often found within structures on shelves or hidden behind objects. Unlike chests, they do not glow or make a sound.
- Random types of ammunition can sometimes be found out in the open, lying on the ground. Sometimes the ammo is alone, but often, it's found in conjunction with a compatible weapon.
- You can often grab a nice assortment of ammunition from a soldier immediately after they've been defeated and eliminated from a match.
- Chests, Supply Drops, and Loot Llamas often contain random collections of ammunition. From the chest shown on the right, seventy-two Medium Bullets are about to be collected, along with a few other useful items, including Bandages.

Keep Your Eyes Peeled for Chests, Supply Drops, Loot Llamas, and Vending Machines

Some weapons and ammo can be found lying out in the open (on the ground).

Throughout the island—mainly within buildings, homes, and other structures, as well as inside of trucks, but sometimes out in the open—you'll discover chests.

Chests have a golden glow and make a sound when you get close to them. Open chests to collect a random selection of weapons, ammo, loot items, and resources. To collect a chest's contents, you must be the first soldier to open it during a match.

Some chests are usually found at the same spot on the map match after match, although this is changing as Epic Games releases new game updates. Sometimes, chests randomly appear during each match, so always be on the lookout for them (and listen carefully for the sound they make).

At random times during a match, you may be lucky enough to spot Supply Drops. These are floating balloons with a wooden crate attached to them. When you spot one, approach with caution, and open the crate. Inside you'll discover a random selection of weapons, loot items, ammo, and resource icons.

Scattered randomly throughout the island are Vending Machines. Exchange resources you've collected to acquire any of the weapons or loot items being offered. Each Vending Machine offers a different selection of items that can be purchased using wood, stone, or metal.

There's Much More You Still Need to Learn

An even rarer object to come across on the island is a Loot Llama. This colorful item looks like a piñata. Open it and you'll discover a collection of random weapons, ammo, loot items, and resource icons. Typically, the weapons found within Loot Llamas are rare and often "legendary."

Now that you understand the core elements of *Fortnite: Battle Royale*, the next step is to download and install the game onto your gaming system, and then customize the game itself, as well as choose the appearance of the soldier you'll be controlling. How to do this is explained within "Section 2—What Every Noob Needs to Know to Get Started Playing."

Then from "Section 3—An 'A to Z' Guide to *Fortnite: Battle Royale*," you'll learn a lot more about exploring, fighting, building, and surviving, as you read an alphabetical listing of detailed entries, each of which relates to something important you need to understand about *Fortnite: Battle Royale*.

SECTION 2

WHAT EVERY NOOB NEEDS TO KNOW TO GET STARTED PLAYING

Before you can start playing *Fortnite: Battle Royale*, you'll need to download and install the game onto your gaming system. Visit www.epicgames.com and click on the Download button to access this screen, which will lead to you to the place online where you can obtain the game for free from Epic Games.

How to Set Up and Link Your Epic Games Account

Before you start playing *Fortnite: Battle Royale*, you'll need to create a free, online-based Epic Games account. Then, if you're a Playstation 4 gamer, you'll need to link your new Epic Games account with your existing PlayStation Network account.

Meanwhile, if you're an Xbox One gamer, you'll need to link your Epic Games account to your paid Xbox Live Gold account, or if you're a Nintendo Switch player, you'll need to link your Epic Games account to your My Nintendo account. Follow these links for directions on how to accomplish this:

- **PlayStation 4 Users**: https://epicgames.helpshift.com/a/fortnite/?p=all&s=fortnite-ps4-support&f=how-do-i-connect-my-psn-account-to-my-epic-account

- **Xbox One Users**: https://epicgames.helpshift.com/a/fortnite/?p=all&s=fortnite-xbox-one-support&f=how-do-i-connect-my-xbox-account-to-my-epic-account
- **Nintendo Switch Users**: https://epicgames.helpshift.com/a/fortnite/?s=fortnite-switch-support&f=how-do-i-connect-my-nintendo-account-to-my-epic-account

If you need to manage your Epic Games account (or you forget your password) visit: www.epicgames.com/fortnite/register.

The Cost of Playing *Fortnite: Battle Royale*

Downloading, installing, and playing the full-version of *Fortnite: Battle Royale* is 100 percent free! However, there are opportunities to make in-game purchases. These are all optional, however.

Things that cost real money when playing *Fortnite: Battle Royale* include buying a Battle Pass; unlocking Battle Pass Tiers; and acquiring outfits, emotes, and related items from the Item Shop.

To acquire a Battle Pass, access the Battle Pass screen, which is accessible from the Lobby, and then select the Purchase button that's displayed near the bottom-left corner of the screen.

After purchasing a Battle Pass, you can option-ally purchase and unlock Battle Pass Tiers, which allow you to obtain the prizes associated with individual Tiers, without first completing the challenges. First, select the Purchase Tier option displayed near the bottom-left corner of the screen.

Choose how many Tiers you want to purchase and unlock at once, and then select the Purchase option. It costs 150 V-Bucks to unlock each Tier. A Battle Pass includes approximately 100 Tiers, depending on the Season.

Purchase emotes that your soldier can show off during a match to express emotion or atti-tude. There are three types of emotes, includ-ing Dance Moves, Graphic Icons, and Spray Paint Tags. Here, the Zany Dance Move is about to be purchased for 500 V-Bucks (about $5.00 US).

Discover What Can Be Done from the Lobby

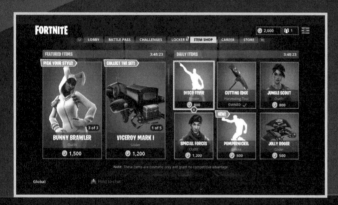

Purchase optional outfits, pickaxe designs, backpack (back bling) designs, and glider designs. These items can be acquired from the Item Shop.

After downloading, installing, and launching the game, you'll find yourself in the Lobby.

From the Lobby, you're able to:

- See your soldier's current appearance in the center of the screen, plus see details about your player level, as well as an overview of daily, weekly, and Tier-based challenges on the left side of the screen.

- Access the Battle Pass, Challenges, Locker, Item Shop, Career, or Store areas before a match.
- Choose a game play mode before a match.
- Access the Game Menu and adjust game-related settings.
- Read important messages from Epic Games (which are sometimes displayed near the bottom-center of the screen).
- Invite online friends to play a Duo or Squads game with you or respond to invites from your online friends.
- Enter into a match by selecting the Play option.

Each of these options will be explained in greater detail within the next section of this guide.

How to Customize Your Game Play Experience

When it comes to adjusting the in-game settings, there are a few that you definitely want to tweak in order to improve your game play experience.

To make these adjustments before any match, from the Lobby, access the game's menu. On a PS4, press the Options button, or on a Nintendo Switch, press the "+" button, for example. From this menu, highlight and select the gear-shaped Settings icon.

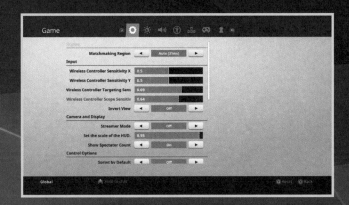

Along the top of the Settings menu are a handful of sub-menu icons. They're labeled: Game, Brightness, Audio, Accessibility, Input, Wireless Controller, and Account. As a noob, leave most of these sub-menu options at their default settings. Just focus on the Audio submenu.

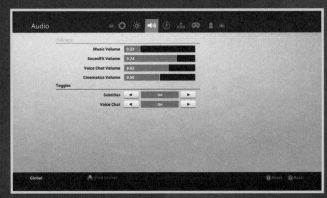

Since sound effects play such a critical role in the game, access the Audio submenu, and then turn down the Music Volume option. Turn up the Sound FX Volume option. If you're using a gaming headset to communicate with other players, also turn up the Voice Chat Volume, and turn on and customize the various Voice Chat features. These options will vary, based on which gaming platform you're using.

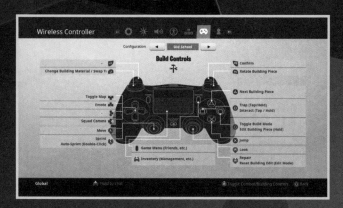

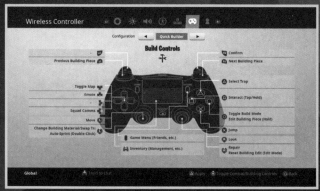

If you're playing *Fortnite: Battle Royale* on a console-based gaming system or have an optional controller connected to your computer, based on your personal gaming style and skill level, choose a Controller Layout that'll work best for you. Your options include: Old School, Quick Builder, Combat Pro, and Builder Pro. PC and Mac gamers can access the game's Input menu and assign a specific game-related function to each keyboard key and mouse button. These controller layouts are for a PS4. Similar options are available from the Xbox One and Nintendo Switch version of the game.

The default controller layout is called Old School. Stick with this one until you've gotten good at playing *Fortnite: Battle Royale* and you've developed your personal play style. If you tend to focus on building, for example, choose the Pro Builder layout. If your focus during matches is mainly fighting, choose the Combat Pro layout. Which you select is purely a matter of personal preference.

At the start of Season 6, it became possible to customize the buttons associated with your controller, as opposed to choosing between one of the four predefined controller layouts. This feature is called key-binding. To select it, access the Controller menu and instead of choosing the Old School, Quick Builder, Builder Pro, or Combat Pro layout, select the Custom option.

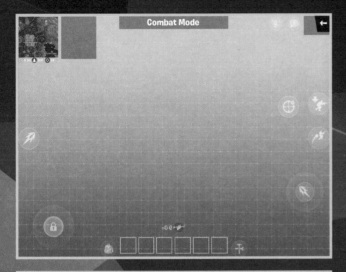

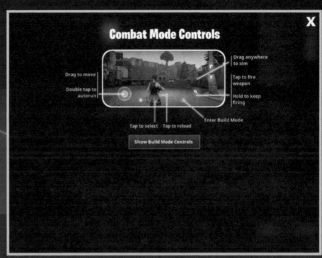

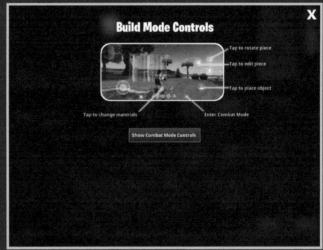

When playing *Fortnite: Battle Royale* on a mobile device, access the HUD Layout Tool to customize the on-screen controls for Combat and Build mode. You're able to customize the size and location of control-related icons that appear on the screen, based on how you hold your smartphone or tablet. Shown here on an iPad Pro.

These are the default on-screen controller layouts for the mobile edition of *Fortnite: Battle Royale*.

Listen Up! Sound Plays an Important Role in *Fortnite: Battle Royale*

While you're playing *Fortnite: Battle Royale*, it's important that you hear all of the game's sound effects clearly. For this reason, you should definitely connect stereo headphones to your gaming system.

If you're playing the Duos, Squads, or a 50 v 50 match, for example, you'll need to communicate with your partner, squad mates, or teammates. To do this, an accessory you'll need is a gaming headset with a built-in microphone. Many companies, like Turtle Beach Corp. (www.turtlebeach.com), offer wired and wireless gaming headsets that work with any gaming system.

Choose Your Soldier's Appearance Before a Match

Prior to each match, you're able to choose the appearance of the soldier you'll be controlling. This is done from the Locker, which is where outfits and optional items you've already purchased or unlocked can be found and managed. To purchase new outfits, back bling, pick axe designs, and emotes, visit the Item Shop.

A growing number of optional outfits allow gamers to use the Edit Style feature to further customize an outfit by unlocking and then selecting outfit variations. These are the style options available for the "Legendary" Carbide outfit.

Emotes Allow You to Showcase Attitude and Personality

While in the pre-deployment area or anytime during a match, you're able to publicly show off some attitude and personality by allowing your character to use one of three types of emotes.

When you choose a graphic icon emote, your soldier tosses an icon into the air for everyone around to see. The icon is displayed for a few seconds and then disappears. There are many different icons that can be unlocked, acquired, or purchased.

Using virtual spray paint, apply a spray paint tag to any flat surface within the game, such as on a wall of any structure. There are many spray paint tags to choose from. Select and use one at a time while visiting the island.

Mix and match a few spray paint designs to create some detailed and colorful graffiti.

The third and most popular type of emote is a dance move. There are hundreds available, although you can only store six at a time.

Showcase one dance move or use two or three back-to-back to demonstrate some lit choreography.

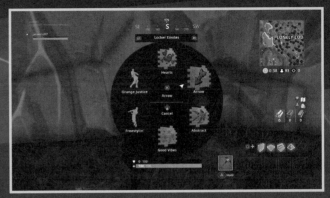

Once you've selected up to six emotes for your soldier, while in the pre-deployment area or during a match, access this Emotes menu to choose and showcase one of the up to six emotes you've preselected. All other nearby players will see it.

Some gamers use emotes during the game as a greeting when they encounter team members or allies. Others use them to taunt adversaries, or to gloat after badly injuring or defeating an enemy. Just remember, when you're using emotes, you can't also use a weapon or build, so your soldier is temporarily vulnerable.

SECTION 3

AN A TO Z GUIDE TO *FORTNITE: BATTLE ROYALE*

tions about how to play *Fortnite: Battle Royale*, and more importantly, questions that relate to how your soldier can stay alive so that you can win #1 Victory Royale.

Well, most of the information you need is offered in this section, along with many tips and strategies that'll help you become a better *Fortnite: Battle Royale* player, regardless of which game play mode you've selected, or which gaming system you're playing on. For easy reference, everything is listed here in alphabetical order.

#1 Victory Royale

At the end of a match, only one soldier survives. As soon as the surviving soldier defeats the last remaining enemy, he/she can perform a victory dance and revel in their success.

This game play mode is unlike any other. Up to 100 gamers are divided into two teams of 50 players each, and the island itself is divided in half. There is a blue team and a red team. You're always on the blue team. As the storm moves, all surviving soldiers are forced toward and ultimately into the circle, where epic battles take place.

Your objective is to help your team defeat all of the enemies on the opposite team. One team wins once everyone on the opposite team has been defeated. Keep in mind, while you're attempting to defeat your enemies, you're also rewarded for helping your teammates.

Most battles between the two teams take place along the border, particularly in or near the circle, which is displayed throughout the match. If you want to start fighting early on, collect weapons, ammo, and loot items right at the start, and head directly into the circle. Keep in mind, during a 50 v 50 match, Supply Drops (shown here) only fall within the circle. These provide a great opportunity to collect the most powerful weapons and loot items.

A

Aim Assist

Available from the Settings menu, Aim Assist makes it easier for players using a wireless controller (as opposed to a keyboard/mouse) to aim weapons in *Fortnite: Battle Royale*. This feature can be turned on (making it easier to aim a weapon) or turned off. Access the Game submenu within Settings, and then scroll down.

Aim Weapon

Anytime you're facing an enemy with a weapon drawn, and you pull the trigger, the bullet travels forward, hopefully hitting your adversary. By pressing the Aim button on the controller (or keyboard/mouse) first, you will zoom in a bit on your target.

It's easier to target enemies, and potentially make a more devastating headshot, if you press the Aim button, target your weapon, and then tap the trigger to fire. Don't just hold down the trigger button unless you're shooting with a machine gun, for example.

If you're using a rifle with a scope (or a thermal scope) when you press the Aim button, this scope view is displayed. It allows you to zoom in on an enemy that's very far away. Use a rifle with a scope for sniping from a distance. You can also use a rifle's scope as binoculars to spy on enemies from a distance, even if you ultimately choose to use explosive weapons to defeat them.

All Terrain Kart (ATK)

An ATK has 400 HP (which could be changed in the future by Epic Games). Each time the vehicle crashes or gets attacked, some of its HP gets depleted. When its HP meter hits zero, the ATK is destroyed.

These souped-up golf carts can be found randomly in many parts of the island, but you're most apt to find them in and around Lazy Links, as well as the desert area that surrounds Paradise Palms, including at the Racetrack (found at map coordinates J6).

One gamer at a time can drive each ATK. Depending on which game play mode you're experiencing, up to three additional soldiers can simultaneously be passengers. (One soldier up front in the passenger seat, and two can stand in the back). While driving, the

However, passengers can shoot or use most loot items while riding in an ATK.

Throughout the island, there's an interconnected network of paved roads and dirt paths you can drive along to get from one place to another. However, an ATK can go off-roading, meaning you can drive almost anywhere on the island, including up mountains and over steep cliffs. ATKs can even go airborne. When they land, the soldiers inside typically won't be injured.

Ambush

When you're within any pre-made building, you always have the option to hide behind furniture or an object, crouch down, aim your weapon, and wait for an enemy to appear. Then, launch a surprise attack to quickly defeat the unsuspecting adversary.

Another way to ambush an opponent is to place Remote Explosives or a Trap somewhere sneaky, where you think an enemy might visit. When he or she gets close, manually detonate the Remote Explosive, or allow the Trap to activate by itself. This will damage or potentially defeat an enemy. To lure an enemy into a booby-trapped area, try dropping a few pieces of valuable loot nearby, using it as bait.

Ammo

All of the different types of guns you'll find on the island require ammunition. A weapon without ammunition is useless. For your more powerful weapons, conserve ammo until situations when that particular weapon is truly needed.

Ammo can be collected from ammo boxes, found and picked up from the ground (shown here), acquired from defeated enemies, and collected from chests or Supply Drops or Loot

Llamas. When you see ammo lying on the ground (out in the open) collect it.

At any time, access the Backpack Inventory screen to see the types of ammo you've collected. Keep in mind, there are different types of ammo, and each works with a specific type of gun, rifle, or weapon. From the Backpack Inventory screen, highlight an ammo type (such as Shells) to determine which weapon that ammo works with, and how much of it you've collected and have on hand (which in this case is eight).

The different types of ammunition include:

- **Heavy Bullets**—Used in sniper rifles and other high-caliber weapons that are designed for long-range shooting.
- **Light Bullets**—Used in pistols, SMGs, and most handheld guns. This type of ammo causes more damage when used at close range. To inflict the most damage, aim for a headshot or hit your target multiple times.
- **Medium Bullets**—Used in assault rifles and similar weapons. This type of ammo is ideal for mid-range shooting, although the closer you are, the more damage each bullet will inflict.
- **Rockets**—This is long-range explosive ammunition that's used with Rocket

Launchers, Guided Missile Launchers, and Grenade Launchers. Even if you don't yet have one of these weapons in your personal arsenal, collect this ammo whenever you can and stockpile it. You can always share it with your teammates. Having a Rocket Launcher, Guided Missile Launcher, and/or a Grenade Launcher will be extremely useful during the End Game.

- **Shells**—Used in shotguns. This ammo will inflict the most damage at close range, but shotguns can be used when you're at any distance from your target. The farther you are away, the less damage each direct hit will inflict.

Ammo Box

Ammo boxes contain a random assortment of ammo. Unlike a chest, an ammo box does not glow. Look for them mainly in homes, buildings, and other pre-made structures. They're often found on shelves (shown here) or under staircases, for example.

Apples

Scattered randomly throughout the island and found under trees, you'll discover Apples. Walk up to an Apple, and when you see the Consume message appear, eat the Apple to replenish 5 HP on your soldier's Health meter. You can eat as many Apples in a row as you can find to boost your soldier's Health meter back up to 100.

You must eat an Apple when and where you find it. You can't pick them up and store them in your backpack for later consumption, like you can with other HP powerups, like Bandages or Med Kits.

Assault Rifles

There are many types of rifles to find and use against your enemies. The rifle type and rarity will determine how powerful it is. Rifles, especially rifles with a scope, are ideal long-range weapons, although they can be used from any distance.

Rifles typically have a slower reload time and hold one (or just a few) rounds of ammo in the chamber. If you miss a first shot, you could become vulnerable to an enemy attack as your weapon reloads (assuming you have more ammo). In between shots, your enemy could also move or take cover. See "DPS Rating," "Fire Rate," "Reload Time," and "Weapon Rarity" for more information about how the damage capabilities and power of weapons are rated in *Fortnite: Battle Royale*.

To see the power and capabilities of a particular rifle (or any weapon), access the Backpack Inventory screen. Details about the highlighted weapon (and the ammo you have available for it) are displayed.

Attic

Many houses and mansions located throughout the island have an attic. It's often within

the attic you'll discover chests (shown), ammo boxes, and/or other powerful loot. Some attics have multiple hidden rooms, so smash through walls, as needed, to explore everywhere.

There are several ways to reach the attic of a house or building. For example, land on a roof of a house, building, tower, or structure after jumping from the Battle Bus, and smash your way down using the pickaxe.

Enter a home or mansion from ground level and work your way upward from inside. (You may need to build a ramp or stairs from the top floor to the attic, and then smash your way through the ceiling using your pickaxe.)

From the outside of a house or mansion, build a ramp from the ground to the roof, climb to the top of the roof, and then use your pickaxe to smash your way down from the roof into the attic.

Auto Material Change

Available from the Settings menu, when turned on, this setting allows you to automatically switch between building materials (wood, stone, or metal) if you run out of the resource you're currently building with, but the structure you're building isn't yet complete. Turning on this feature could save you valuable seconds while in Building mode.

Anytime you enter Building mode, after selecting which building tile you want to create, select between wood, stone, or metal as your building material. You're able to keep building as long as you have an ample supply of that material. When you run out, you'll need to switch building materials (either automatically or manually) or go collect additional resources before you can continue building.

B

Back Bling

From the Locker, one of the customizations you can make to your soldier is the style of their back bling (backpack). The back bling you choose determines its appearance but has no impact on what it can hold or how it's used within the game. Many outfits are sold with matching back bling.

You're able to customize the appearance of your soldier before every match. From the Lobby, select the Locker. To change the back bling, highlight and select the Back Bling option. It's found below the Account and Equipment heading.

One of the new types of back bling added to the game at the start of Season 6 was virtual pets that can be unlocked and carried in a back-

Once you access the Back Bling menu, all of the different backpack styles you've unlocked, purchased, or collected thus far are displayed. You can purchase new back bling designs from the Item Shop; unlock back bling by accomplishing daily, weekly, or Battle Pass–related goals or challenges; or by acquiring this type of loot from a free Twitch Prime Pack, for example. (See "Twitch Prime Pack" for more info on these free downloads.)

Backpack

Every soldier carries a backpack. Within it are six slots for carrying a pickaxe, along with five different types of weapons or loot items. A backpack also holds all of the ammo you find and pick up during a match.

From the Backpack Inventory screen, you're able to rearrange the contents of what's inside, so you can make your most useful weapons and items available to you the quickest. Deciding what types of weapons and ammo you'll carry within your backpack at any given time is an important decision. As a match progresses, your needs will definitely change.

The contents of your backpack are displayed in the lower-right corner of the PS4 screen throughout each match. Its position may vary, depending on which gaming platform you're using.

Once the slots in your backpack are filled up, if you want to swap out an item, select and hold what you want to get rid of, and then grab the new item. The item you were holding will be dropped, and the new one will be picked up. (Notice the Backpack Full message displayed at the top of the Burst Assault Rifle banner.)

To share a weapon, loot item, or resources with a partner, squad mate, or teammate, from the Backpack Inventory screen, select what you want to share with the soldier when you're close to him or her, and then drop the selected weapon, ammo, loot item, or resources at their feet for them to pick up.

Within your backpack, it's also a good idea to hold onto at least one type of HP powerup item that will help to keep your soldier alive if he or she gets injured. Bandages, Cozy Campfires, Chug Jugs, Med Kits, and Slurp Juice are some of the more useful pieces of loot that will help you replenish your soldier's Health (HP) meter.

Backpack Inventory

This is the combination of weapons, loot, and ammo that you're carrying around at any given time. In addition to your pickaxe, your backpack has six inventory slots. Each slot can hold one weapon or loot item. It's possible to hold multiples of some loot items, such as Bandages, within a single slot.

At any time, you can drop an item from your backpack in order to pick up something different. For example, once your backpack is filled, you can drop a pistol to pick up a shotgun. Or if you have a few Bandages, you might want to use or drop them, so you can pick up and carry a more powerful Med Kit or Chug Jug that you find.

If you have two of the same type of gun that has a long re-load time, for example, place them in side-by-side slots within your backpack. Then, when one weapon needs to reload, instead of waiting (and being vulnerable to attack), immediately switch to the other weapon.

Bandages

Bandages can be found within chests, lying on the ground (often within houses, buildings, or structures), collected from defeated enemies, or found within Supply Drops or Loot Llamas, for example. Each time you use a Bandage, it replenishes 15 HP (up to 100). Within one backpack slot, you can hold up to five Bandages, and then use them individually when they're needed.

It takes several seconds to use Bandages, during which time your soldier will be vulnerable to attack, since he/she can't move, fire a weapon, or build at the same time. Consider crouching behind an object or building walls around your soldier for protection before using Bandages or consuming any health- and/or shield-replenishing item.

Basement

Located within many homes, buildings, mansions, and other structures are basements. It's here (and in attics) that you'll often find chests and powerful weapons, as well as useful ammo and loot.

Outside of a home, if you see a cellar door, smash it open with your pickaxe, enter into the basement, and explore. Be sure to look for hidden rooms. From within some homes, buildings, mansions, and other structures, you'll need to smash through the floor when you're at ground level in order to discover a hidden basement.

Basketball

Scattered throughout the island, mainly within points of interest, including Paradise Palms, you'll come across basketball courts. If you want to take a break from combat and exploration to shoot some hoops, you must first unlock the Basketball emote and add it to your soldier's Emotes menu before a match. This is done from the Locker.

During a match, when you find a basketball court, position your soldier on the court where you want to shoot from.

Select the Basketball emote from the Emotes menu.

Your soldier will toss the basketball toward the net. Reposition your soldier as needed to score some baskets. Keep in mind, while you're playing basketball, your soldier is out in the open and vulnerable to attack. Be ready to grab a weapon or build in order to defend yourself.

Battle Bus

At the start of a match you'll find yourself (along with other soldiers) waiting in the pre-deployment area. Feel free to walk around and explore while waiting to board the Battle Bus, which will transport everyone to the island.

The Battle Bus is a blue bus that flies. It'll take you (and up to 99 other soldiers) from the pre-deployment area directly over the island.

Battle Bus Route

While in the pre-deployment area waiting for the Battle Bus, or once aboard it, press the Map button to access the island map. During this period, a blue line, comprised of arrows, is displayed. This line shows the random route that the bus will follow as it travels over the island. Study this map to choose the ideal moment to jump out of the Battle Bus, based on your desired landing location.

Battle Pass

In conjunction with each season, Epic Games offers a new Battle Pass for sale. This is a collection of approximately 100 Tier-based challenges. Each time you complete a challenge your soldier gains Experience Points (XP) and unlocks a prize, such as a character customization item.

Each Battle Pass lasts for one gaming season (between two and three months). To acquire a Battle Pass, view its Tiers, and see what loot items and prizes can be unlocked by completing each Tier, from the Lobby, select the Battle Pass option.

Once you have enough V-Bucks, visit the Battle Pass screen and select the Purchase Battle Pass option. After purchasing and activating a Battle Pass, if you can't (or don't want to) complete the necessary challenges to unlock the prizes being offered, for an additional fee, consider purchasing individual Battle Pass Tiers. Each Tier you unlock with a purchase (at a cost of 150 V-Bucks) will unlock the prize(s) offered in that Tier.

If you don't want to purchase a Battle Pass, you can continue playing *Fortnite: Battle Royale* for free, but the rewards for completing daily or weekly challenges, or reaching certain Experience Levels, will not be as rare or as exciting as what you'd unlock with a purchased Battle Pass.

Battle Pass Tier

Each Tier of a Battle Pass consists of a series of pre-defined challenges. Access the Battle Pass screen (from the Lobby) to view each Tier and see what will be unlocked by completing

Boogie Bomb

This type of weapon can be collected and stored within your backpack. When you opt to use it, toss it directly at an enemy soldier. They'll be forced to dance for five seconds, during which time they'll receive damage.

Bouncer Pad

Depending on how and where you position this item, you can use it to catapult your soldier into the air in order to quickly reach a different location, or you can use it to send your enemies bouncing up and down, or back and forth in a loop. This item gets stored with your resources (and becomes available within Building mode once one or more of them are acquired). Place a Bouncer Pad on a wall or ceiling within a structure, for example.

If you jump onto the back of an All Terrain Kart, this too serves as a Bouncer Pad.

Builder Pro Controller Layout

From the Settings menu, select the Wireless Controller option. You're then able to choose between several pre-configured controller layouts. The Builder Pro layout is ideal for a player who has expertise in building and uses this capability as one of their main strategies. This controller layout makes the most popular building tools more readily accessible.

Building Mode

One of the keys to becoming a pro *Fortnite: Battle Royale* player is to be able to quickly switch into and out of Building mode. While in Building mode, you must be able to quickly construct forts or structures without thinking too much about it.

The faster you build, the bigger your advantage will be, especially if you're in the midst of a firefight and you're building a ramp or fortress to get higher than your opponent, or for protection (shielding) from an incoming attack.

Using the ramp/stairs piece, quickly build tall ramps/stairs to help you reach otherwise inaccessible areas within a building or structure. You can also create a ramp or stairs to quickly climb up higher than your opponent during a firefight. Typically, the soldier who is higher up has a tactical advantage.

Once a wall or ceiling piece has been built or you've constructed a fortress, for example, enter into Edit mode to add a window or door to the structure.

Once in Building mode, choose which building piece(s) to create or edit, as well as which resource to build with. Wood is the fastest but offers the least protection. Metal takes longer to build with but offers the most protection. This is what a single vertical wall piece (made of wood) looks like as it's being built.

Use a door to easily enter/exit a structure. Keep in mind, once you build a door, anyone can pass through it, whether they're invited or not. Use a window to see out of or shoot from. Of course, an enemy can see in through a window and shoot at you as well.

Building Techniques

Some *Fortnite: Battle Royale* players spend countless hours practicing in Building mode, to master how to construct elaborate, multi-level fortresses. Others rely more on their fighting and combat skills and utilize Building mode only when it's absolutely essential.

Learn to Quickly Build 1x1 Fortresses

A 1x1 fortress is simply four walls around you, with a ramp in the center, that goes up multiple levels. Using wood allows you to build with the greatest speed, but using metal offers the best protection. Keep practicing until you're able to build this type of fortress very quickly, without having to think too much about it.

One type of structure you definitely want to learn how to build is a 1x1 fortress.

Building Tiles

After activating Building mode, choose which resource (wood, stone, or metal) you want to build with, and then choose which building piece you want to create. Here, the available building pieces are displayed near the bottom-right corner of the screen, but this will vary based on which gaming platform you're using.

The key to becoming an expert at building is being able to mix and match building pieces to construct durable and useful structures, ramps, bridges, or fortresses, whenever and wherever they're needed. The structure shown here was built using wood, stone, and metal. You can see that each material looks different by studying this structure.

The building pieces and structures you can construct are based mainly on how much resources you've collected and your own creativity. Once you get into the End Game phase of a match, you'll discover your adversaries will typically build tall and often highly creative fortresses—both for protection, and from which they launch their final assaults.

Here's how to build a 1x1 fortress:

If the ground is not flat, or you're building on top of an existing structure, create and place one floor/ceiling tile on the ground.

Build four vertical walls so they surround you.

In the center, build a ramp. As the ramp is being constructed, jump on it.

Keep repeating this process to add levels to your fort.

At the top, consider adding four pyramid-shaped roof pieces around the roof for added protection when you peek out. However, if you need protection from directly above as well, be sure to add a roof over your soldier's head.

In many instances, height is more important than security. Build a quick and tall ramp upwards, and then shoot down at enemies below.

Add a vertical wall on both sides of the ramp (near the top) to provide more protection when you're standing at the top and shooting at enemies below you. As long as an enemy does not have time to shoot and destroy your ramp while you're on it, you'll be at an advantage. It's safe for your soldier to fall three stories maximum when leaping out or off of a structure. If he/she falls from any higher, injury (or worse) will result.

If a soldier shoots and destroys just one tile that's located near the bottom of a ramp, the entire ramp will come crashing down, along with whoever is standing on the ramp.

While it'll take more resources, consider building more complex ramps (like these) out

of stone or metal. They'll last longer against a direct attack.

When you need quick protection, build a vertical wall with the strongest material you have available, and then quickly build a ramp (or stairs) directly behind it. You can then crouch down directly behind this structure for protection. Doing this provides a double layer of shielding that an enemy will have to shoot through and destroy in order to reach you. By crouching down, you become a smaller target.

In some cases, building two ramps, side-by-side, gives you an advantage. First, an opponent below can't see your soldier's exact location when you move back and forth between ramps. Also, if one ramp is about to get destroyed, quickly leap to the other to survive the attack and avoid falling. Yes, this requires more resources, but it's often worth it.

An Over-Under Ramp allows you to build a ramp below your soldier's feet, and at the same time, place ramp tiles over your soldier's head. This will help to protect against attacks from above as you're building a ramp to get higher up.

Buildings & Structures Found on the Island

Throughout the island, you'll find many houses and mansions to explore, and potentially hide or fight within. On the outside, the homes and mansions may all look different. However, on the inside, all offer several levels, and on each level, you'll discover multiple rooms and hallways to explore. Some homes, for example, also have an attic and/or basement.

In addition to homes and mansions, various points of interest on the island also offer tall buildings, farm houses, factories, mines, indoor sports arenas, stores, restaurants, gas stations, water towers (shown here), watch towers, churches, and other types of pre-created structures.

Anytime you're about to enter a building, listen carefully for movement coming from the inside. You might hear an enemy's footsteps, doors opening/closing, or an adversary using their pickaxe to smash things. Whatever the case, if you hear movement and still choose to enter that structure, do so with your weapon drawn. Also consider tiptoeing, so you generate less noise.

Before entering a building, peek through the window, if possible. If you see an enemy, shoot through the window or toss a Grenade.

Almost any building or structure you discover on the island can be smashed using a pickaxe and used to collect resources. This includes the walls, floors, and ceilings, as well as any contents inside (such as furniture or machinery).

When you approach a house, building, or structure and see the door is already open, this means someone is currently inside, or has already searched that structure and has left. If they're still inside, consider waiting outside, so you can launch a surprise attack, defeat the enemy as they leave, and collect all of their weapons, ammo, loot, and resources. If you choose to enter the structure, do so with extreme caution and with your weapon drawn. You'll likely encounter one or more enemies inside and be forced into a firefight within a confined space.

If you know an enemy is hiding within a building and you have a projectile explosive weapon at your disposal (or some type of Grenade or Remote Explosive), use that weaponry to blow up the building and whoever is inside. Here, instead of walking through the front door, a soldier is about to shoot a guided missile through the open front door. The resulting explosion will destroy much of the house (and likely injure or defeat whoever is inside).

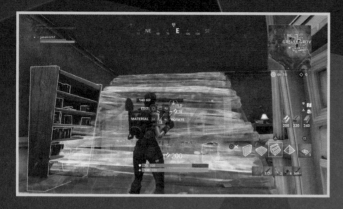

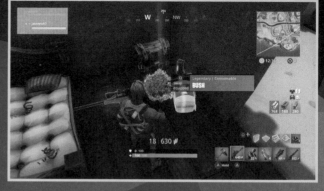

Regardless of the building or structure you're in, use Building mode to build inside. For example, build a vertical wall inside a building for protection or to block a staircase or entranceway. Build a ramp (or stairs) to help you reach an otherwise inaccessible area inside an existing structure.

Bush

Use a bush as a hiding spot. Walk up to it and crouch down inside. Depending on the size of the bush, you can go unseen by nearby enemies. However, if you do get spotted, the bush offers zero protection from incoming weapon fire.

It's also possible to find and collect a Bush loot item. This is a loot item you can carry with you in your backpack until it's needed.

When you use it, your soldier will wear the bush as camouflage in order to blend in with their outdoor surroundings. Crouch down so you remain unseen. This is the view you'll see when your soldier is wearing a Bush loot item.

While wearing a Bush loot item, you're able to move around freely. However, when an enemy spots a moving bush, they'll attack it. With the Bush loot item active, crouch down. You're able to target and shoot a weapon from within the bush. Remember, if someone shoots back, the bush offers zero protection.

Bush Camping

Bush camping is a strategy where you simply hide in a bush (in the safe area of the circle), waiting for the other enemy soldiers to battle and defeat each other, while your soldier remains safely hidden until the End Game portion of a match.

When you hide within a bush, or use the Bush camouflage item, you are almost entirely hidden, even when an enemy comes close to your location. During the End Game, when the circle is very small and you can't find one or more of your remaining enemies, shoot at the bushes in the immediate area. This is a popular hiding spot.

C

Chests

Once you locate a chest, walk up and open it. Depending on its location, you may need to crouch down to open a chest. The chest's contents will scatter out on the ground. Based on what you already have within your backpack, pick and choose the weapons, ammo, loot, and resource items you want to grab, and if necessary, replace unwanted items in your backpack with new ones.

When you're exploring a building or area, listen carefully for the special sound a chest makes as you get close to it, and always be on the lookout for their golden glow.

Sometimes, to reach a chest that's hidden within a building or structure, you'll need to build a ramp or stairs to reach it. If a chest is hidden in an attic, it may be necessary to get to the outside roof and then use your pickaxe to smash downward (through the roof) into the attic.

If you're inside a house and can't figure out how to reach the attic, go to the top floor and build a ramp to the ceiling. Use your pickaxe to smash upward through the ceiling.

Sometimes, you'll discover chests sitting out in the open, or they could be hidden inside or behind something. Here, a chest was found in the back of a pickup truck and another was hidden within a dog house.

Throughout the island, the location of chests is often the same from match to match. So, once you find a chest, remember its location. During a future match, return to that location and open the chest to collect what's inside. In some of the island's points of interest, the location of the chests is somewhat random. Once a chest is opened during a match, it rarely respawns. The first soldier to reach and open a chest is the one who receives its contents.

If you choose to approach a chest that's out in the open, do so with extreme caution. There could be an enemy soldier armed with a sniper rifle waiting for you to approach the chest. As soon as you're seen, you'll get shot. Be prepared to quickly build barrier walls around yourself for protection as you open a chest that's located in a spot that makes you vulnerable to attack.

Chiller

While a Chiller is shaped like a Trap, it's more of a survival and transportation tool that doesn't do any harm. Once it's activated, any soldier who steps on it will have their feet transformed into ice blocks. They can then slide for great distances along the ground and travel faster than running until the ice thaws. A Chiller must be placed on a flat surface. Thus, you'll often need to first build a floor tile (made from wood, stone, or metal) and then place the Chiller on top of it.

Chug Jug

When you consume a Chug Jug, your Health *and* Shield meters get replenished to 100 percent. A Chug Jug takes 15 seconds to consume. During this time, your soldier can't move around, build, or fire a weapon. They're vulnerable to attack. Before consuming a Chug Jug, find a secluded or secure location.

Drink a Chug Jug early in a match to fully charge your Health and Shields meters, and then save at least one or two until the End Game portion of a match, when survival becomes more difficult and having 100 percent health and shields will keep you alive longer.

Circle

The area within the outer circle of the island map is currently the safe (inhabitable) area of the island. This area has not yet been ravaged by the storm. The area in pink is the uninhabitable area, where the storm is already active.

When you see two circles on a map, the area within the outer circle is currently the safe area. The area within the inner circle shows you the impact the storm will have the next time it expands and moves. A white line indicates the most direct route to follow so that you stay out of the storm.

Clingers

These explosive weapons look like a toilet plunger and can be collected and stored in your soldier's backpack. When you want to use one, select it as the active weapon, and then toss it directly at your enemy or any nearby object.

Once a Clinger is thrown, it will stick directly to an enemy soldier or nearby object (such as a wall or tree). It will turn blue, indicating it's been activated. Then, within a few seconds,

it'll automatically explode! Anyone caught in the explosion will be injured (or worse).

Clingers will stick to almost anything, and once they've attached to a soldier or object, they can't be removed. To increase the damage these explosive weapons cause, quickly throw two or more of them at the same target, and then take cover!

Combat Mode

When in Combat mode your soldier is holding a weapon (any type of gun), or an item (such as a Grenade or Remote Explosives) that can be used as a weapon. Once two or more weapons are stored within slots of your backpack, you can easily switch between them. It's only possible to have one active weapon (in your soldier's hands) at a time. Thus, organizing your backpack, so you can quickly grab whichever weapon you need, is essential.

While you'll have the best aim if you crouch down before targeting and firing your weapon, you can use a weapon while you're standing up, walking, running, crouching, jumping, or tiptoeing. However, the faster you're moving, the worse your aim will be.

During those first few seconds when you land on the island and you're unarmed, or anytime you run out of ammo and find yourself in close proximity to an enemy, you have two choices. First, you can go on the offensive and use your pickaxe as a short-range weapon. Each successful hit will do a small amount of damage to your opponent, so you'll need to whack 'em multiple times for the attack to be fatal. Your second option is simply to run and try to avoid being shot at as you leave the area.

Combat Pro Controller Layout

If your primary strategy when playing *Fortnite: Battle Royale* is combat, and you're playing on a PS4, Xbox One, or Nintendo Switch, consider switching your wireless controller layout to Combat Pro. This makes the most commonly used fighting features more readily available to you. From the Lobby, access the Settings menu, and then choose the Wireless Controller submenu.

Contrail

This is the animation you see trailing behind your soldier as he/she freefalls from the Battle Bus toward the island. You're able to unlock a wide range of contrail designs and patterns. These soldier customization items typically can't be purchased from the Item Shop. They must be unlocked by completing challenges or acquired (from a Twitch Prime Pack, for example).

Cozy Campfire

Cozy Campfires are rare, but when you find one, save it for when you, or you and your allies (if you're playing Duos or Squad mode) need healing. Collect a Cozy Campfire from chests, Supply Drops, or defeated enemies, and then store it in your backpack until it's needed.

To activate a Cozy Campfire, you must be on a flat surface, so consider entering into Building mode, and creating one floor tile, especially if you're outdoors. Select and activate the Cozy Campfire, and then stand directly next to the flame. For each second you're close to the flame (for up to 25 seconds), your Health meter increases by 2 HP.

Since it'll take you at least 30 seconds to set up and reap the full benefits of a Cozy Campfire, and you're vulnerable to attack while you're using it, build four walls around yourself for added protection, or make sure you're in a secluded and secure area. Any of your allies that also stand next to the flame will have their HP increased as well. Place two Cozy Campfires on top of each other to double the HP-boosting benefit.

Crouch

At any time, your soldier has the ability to crouch down. Do this to hide behind an object to make yourself a smaller target. When you crouch down and move around, this allows you to tiptoe. You'll move slower but make a lot less noise.

As you're exploring indoor areas where enemies may be lurking, tiptoeing around makes it much harder for someone to hear you approaching and makes you a smaller target if you're spotted. There will be times when you need to crouch down in order to pass under an object or open a chest (or ammo box), based on where it's positioned.

Regardless of what type of weapon you're using, when you crouch down before aiming and firing that weapon, your accuracy improves.

Customization HUD Tool (*Fortnite* Mobile)

If you're playing *Fortnite: Battle Royale* on an iPhone, iPad, or Android-based smartphone or tablet, you have the ability to fully customize the touchscreen controls.

To access the Customization HUD menu, from the Lobby screen, tap on the menu icon that's located in the top-right corner of the screen. It looks like three horizontal lines. From the menu, tap on the HUD Layout Tool option. Then, using your finger, drag the various control icons around on the screen, and place each of them, one at a time, in the desired location.

Based on how you hold your mobile device, for both Combat and Build modes, choose the ideal location and size for each icon. This is a matter of personal preference. Choose a location for each icon that's easy for you to reach, and that's intuitive, without having to look around on the screen when you're engaged in a match.

Press the left pointing arrow icon in the top-right corner of the screen to access commands for adjusting the size of each icon. When you're done, tap again on the left-pointing arrow icon that's displayed in the top-right corner of the screen. To save your changes, tap on the Save and Exit button. Your new screen layout will remain active until you manually change or reset it.

Customized Controls

If you're playing *Fortnite: Battle Royale* on a console-based gaming system, such as the PS4, Xbox One, or Nintendo Switch, to customize the wireless controller layout, access the Controller menu.

To do this, from the Lobby, access the Settings menu. On the PS4, for example, press the Options button to access the main menu, and then highlight and select the gear-shaped Settings menu. From the Settings menu, scroll to the Controller submenu. Choose a wireless controller layout.

If you're playing *Fortnite: Battle Royale* on a Windows PC or Mac and using a keyboard and mouse instead of a controller, from the Settings menu, choose the Input submenu. You can then associate specific keyboard keys or mouse controls with specific commands and movements available within the game. For most players, however, the default settings work very well, so there's no need to tinker with these settings.

Once you make changes to the controller or keyboard/mouse layout, be sure to save your changes. To reset the active layout to their default settings, choose the Restore option that's displayed near the bottom of the Wireless Controller menu screen.

Whatever controller or keyboard/mouse layout you select, memorize that layout so you can quickly access important features, move your soldier around, or switch between fighting and building mode, for example. If you waste valuable seconds trying to figure out which button to press in order to achieve something, you'll wind up getting defeated by an opponent in no time.

D

Daily Items

Every day, Epic Games offers a new selection of outfits and related character customization items (such as limited edition back bling or pickaxe designs). These are made available for sale from the Item Shop. The items sold within the Item Shop are typically only available for a short time.

Access the Item Shop from the Lobby. On the left side of the screen, you'll see one or two featured outfits or items (each sold separately). A graphic showing what an outfit looks like, its name, as well as its price (in V-Bucks) is displayed within a rectangular box. If you want to purchase it, highlight and select the box.

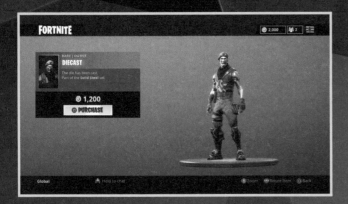

You'll be asked to confirm your purchase decision, assuming you have enough V-Bucks to make the purchase. (You can purchase additional V-Bucks, using real money, from the Shop). Here, the Diecast outfit is about to be purchased for 1,200 V-Bucks. It does not come with matching back bling.

In conjunction with each new outfit, a matching backpack (back bling design) is sometimes included but considered a separate item. A matching glider and pickaxe design may also be offered but sold separately. In addition to the featured outfit(s) and/or items, to the right, you'll notice a section of six additional items, labeled Daily Items, each of which can be purchased separately.

The Daily Items might include additional (optional) outfits, as well as pickaxe or glider designs. Often, at least one or two new emotes are also offered for sale. Again, all of the customization options for your character are for appearance purposes only. None actually give your soldier a competitive advantage during a match. However, altering your soldier's appearance can make him or her look truly unique.

Once an outfit, back bling design, glider design, or emote is purchased and unlocked, it becomes available within your Locker.

Access the Locker from the Lobby to choose the appearance of your soldier before a match, using outfits and items that you've previously purchased, acquired, or unlocked.

Damage Rating

This is a numeric rating, based on how much potential damage a weapon can cause per direct hit. Always choose an appropriate type of weapon for the task at hand, and one with the highest Damage Rating available to you.

Every weapon offered in *Fortnite: Battle Royale* is categorized by type, and then rated in a variety of ways so gamers can more easily determine the impact it'll have on opponents when used.

Once you've selected a weapon to carry, access the Backpack Inventory screen to see detailed information about that particular weapon and how much ammunition you have available for it. Only do this when your soldier is secure, and not vulnerable to an enemy attack.

Dance Moves

This is one of three types of emotes that allow your soldier to express himself or herself while in the pre-deployment area or anytime during a match. Many different dance moves can be unlocked and used. Create your own elaborate choreography by mixing and matching dance move emotes. Use them to distract enemies, brag after a win, or entertain onlookers. From the Emotes menu, a dance move has been selected and will be performed by this soldier.

Defeat Opponent

Each time you engage an enemy soldier in battle and win, he or she will be defeated and eliminated from the match. At that time, all of the weapons, ammo, loot, and resources the soldier was carrying drops to the ground and becomes available for you (or anyone else in the area) to take.

Upgrading your arsenal with weapons, ammo, and loot from defeated enemies potentially gives you access to more powerful items than what you previously had at your disposal. Plus, when you collect a defeated enemy's resources, this saves you a lot of time, since you won't have to harvest as much wood, stone, and metal yourself.

Defeating enemies is one of the fastest ways to increase your character's Experience Level, since this will earn you Experience Points (XP).

DPS Rating

DPS stands for "Damage Per Second." Use this rating to help estimate a weapon's power and damage capabilities. It does not consider things like accuracy of your aim, or the extra damage you can inflict by making a headshot, for example. In general, DPS is calculated by multiplying the damage the weapon can cause (its Damage Rating) by its Fire Rate.

The rarity of a weapon contributes heavily to its Damage Per Second (DPS) rating. Thus, the DPS rating for a "legendary" weapon is much higher than the DPS rating for an identical weapon that has a "common" rarity. See "Weapon Rarity" for more information.

Duos Game Play Mode

Like Solo and Squads, this is one of *Fortnite: Battle Royale*'s game play modes that's always available.

From the Lobby, highlight and select the Game Play Mode option displayed above the Play option, and then choose which Game Play Mode you want to experience.

Select Duos mode to team up with one friend and confront up to 98 other opponents. The friend you select must be an active *Fortnite: Battle Royale* player who is currently online and connected to the game. If you plan to invite a friend, select the "Don't Fill" option after selecting Duos mode.

After selecting Duos mode, you can choose your partner, or have the game assign you a random partner by selecting the "Fill" option. Once you and your partner are working together, communication throughout the match is essential. Ideally, you both want to be using a gaming headset, so you can communicate with each other using your voices.

Another way to communicate with other gamers during a match is using the Quick Chat menu. Access it anytime while in the pre-deployment area or on the island during a match. From here, you can send the equivalent of an instant message to your team members. Messages include: "Enemy Spotted," "Need Weapon," "Need Materials," "Need Shields," and "Need Meds."

Dusty Divot

In the early days of *Fortnite: Battle Royale*, this point of interest was called Dusty Dunes. It then become a research facility during Season

4, called Dusty Divot. As Season 6 kicked off, this area (which can be found at map coordinates G5) once again got a makeover.

The research facility has been mostly destroyed, but a few buildings and structures still remain. Because Dusty Divot is centrally located on the map, it is one of the more popular points of interest in the game (especially if you're playing a 50 v 50 match).

Behind each closed door, you may find a destroyed laboratory or office that's filled with useful items to collect, or you could discover an enemy soldier waiting to pummel you with their weapons, so be prepared for whatever you encounter, and keep your weapon drawn.

E

Emotes

While you're in the pre-deployment area, or anytime during a match while you're on the island, you can communicate with your adversaries using three types of emotes.

Emotes must first be unlocked or purchased, and then added to your customized Emotes menu from the Locker prior to any match. The Emotes menu has six slots. After unlocking various types of emotes, choose which one goes into each slot. Emotes can be unlocked by purchasing them, by completing challenges or Battle Pass Tiers, or by acquiring them through promotions.

End Game

The End Game is the portion of a match that takes place during the final minutes, when the circle has become extremely small, and only a few highly skilled soldiers remain alive.

Instead of relying on the safety of a fort, many gamers opt to rush their enemies and engage in close-to-mid-range firefights to finish off their final opponents during an End Game.

Another option is to rush an enemy's fortress and attack with whatever explosive weapons and guns you have available and that are suited for a close-to-mid-range attack. Alternatively, from a distance, rely on a Grenade Launcher, Rocket Launcher, and/or a Guided Missile Launcher to blow up and destroy an enemy's fort (or any structure), and hopefully take out the enemy as well.

It's during the End Game that some gamers opt to build a tall and study fortress, which they'll use for protection, and from which they'll launch their attacks using projectile weapons and long-range weapons.

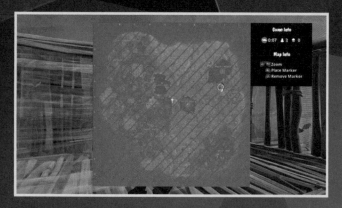

Some more gutsy gamers opt to rush enemy forts, using guns, Grenades, Clingers, or whatever weapons are at their disposal as they launch a close-range attack. During the final moments of the End Game, expect the circle to be very small. In fact, you may literally find yourself on top of or below your opponent(s). Having the height advantage almost always works better.

Go into the final circle with your Health and Shield meters fully charged. Plus, have plenty of resources on hand (up to 1,000 wood, stone, and/or metal is ideal). It's also necessary to have the right assortment of weapons in your arsenal. A Grenade Launcher, Guided Missile Launcher, and/or Rocket Launcher, as well as a Sniper Rifle (or rifle with a scope) are definitely must have weapons if you plan to launch long-range attacks.

Since Epic Games has been tweaking the game a bit, building fortresses during the End Game is less important than it used to be. You can survive within the Final Circle by relying on short-range or mid-range weapons, and/or explosives, to help you rush enemies and launch fierce attacks.

Experience Points (XP)

There are many ways to earn XP during a match, including just participating in matches (and not leaving a match early). The longer you stay alive, the more XP you receive. You also receive XP for successful enemy attacks (i.e., causing damage to an enemy), and for each enemy soldier you actually defeat.

XP (or an XP Modifier) can also be earned by completing certain daily, weekly, or Battle Pass-related challenges. By unlocking an XP Modifier, you will receive bonus XP during each match for the remainder of the Battle Pass Tier (or the entire Battle Pass).

Earning XP helps you to increase your Experience Level, which is displayed in the Lobby. One way to see the impact an XP Modifier is having on your success is to access the Profile screen. To reach it from the Lobby, select the Career option, and then highlight and select the Profile option.

Exploration

During any match, one of your primary objectives is exploration of the island. Depending on your strategy, this might mean visiting one or more points of interest, and then exploring each of the homes, buildings, and/or structures in that area.

Exploration could also mean searching the less-popular areas of the island, in the outskirts of the various points of interest. Collect weapons, ammo, loot, and resources you discover lying on the ground, out in the open, or within the random buildings and structures you encounter.

Like everything else on the island, exploration can be dangerous. Avoid accidently falling off a cliff or tower, for example. Any fall from higher than three stories could be fatal. Falls from lower heights, however, often cause HP damage. Shields do not protect a soldier from falls.

Instead of jumping off of a tall and steep cliff, you can safely slide down.

Especially if there are enemy soldiers in the same vicinity as you on the island, it's always a good idea to stay on higher ground. If you're

on the roof of a building, and you want to reach the roof of a neighboring building, instead of going down to ground level, entering the other building, and then climbing back up in the second building, consider building a bridge between the roofs of the two buildings.

The quickest way to travel across water, such as the lake area of Loot Lake, is to build a bridge and walk across it. Walking through water is a slow process, and it leaves you out in the open and vulnerable to attack.

Anytime you're exploring inside of a home, building, or structure, your soldier will make noise. If you know enemies are in the immediate area, tiptoe around, and avoid smashing objects with your pickaxe.

Also, whenever you open or close a door, this too makes a sound that can be heard by others who are nearby. To confuse or mislead your enemies, consider closing doors behind you after you open and pass through them.

One of the best ways to get a bird's eye view of an area is to quickly build a tall ramp, climb to the top, and look around. If there are enemies in the area, they'll definitely see the ramp, so be prepared to take cover or shoot at them.

When you see an enemy at the top of a tall ramp, one strategy is to attempt to destroy the bottom of that ramp, so the whole thing comes crashing down. (Remember, a fall from a great height will cause a soldier to perish.)

Anytime you're out in the open and need to travel a great distance, run fast, in a zigzag and unpredictable formation, and keep jumping in order to make yourself a more difficult target to hit.

The fastest way to get around the island is to drive (or ride as a passenger) within an ATK (shown on the left). Other transportation options include: riding a Shopping Cart (shown on the right), using a Jetpack (when available within the game), building and stepping onto a Launch Pad, walking into a Rift, or stepping on a Bouncer Pad.

Inside the large barn, you'll discover haystacks. While you can crouch down and hide behind them, this offers no protective shielding. By smashing or shooting at the hay, you'll sometimes discover useful goodies. However, there could just as easily be an enemy soldier waiting to launch an attack from behind a haystack. It's also possible to stand on haystacks, so you can be a bit higher than ground level (to give yourself a tactical and visual advantage).

These massive, head-shaped statues typically have two or three chests lying next to them. You'll discover these stone heads scattered around the island, so keep your eyes peeled.

 F

Fatal Fields

Found at map coordinates G8.5, this is one of the island's farming areas. The farmhouse, silos, barn, and stable, as well as the farm's other structures, are far apart from each other. To reach each of them, you'll need to spend time out in the open and will be vulnerable to attack. Be prepared to hide behind objects, or build walls to use as shields, in case you're attacked.

Search the large farmhouse carefully. Inside the bathroom, smash your way into this hidden room. It often contains a chest.

When Fatal Fields is one of the first or last points of interest the Battle Bus passes over, it tends to become even more crowded than usual, which means you're more apt to encounter enemy soldiers and be forced to fight.

There are two silos on this farm. Land on the top of one and then smash your way down. Inside you'll likely find a chest, or potentially other useful weapons, ammo, or loot. It's also possible to smash the silos from the ground using your soldier's pickaxe.

Fire Rate

When it comes to determining how powerful a weapon is, its Fire Rate refers to the number of bullets (or ammo rounds) the weapon can fire per second. Some of the most powerful weapons have a slow Fire Rate, so to inflict the most damage, your aim needs to be perfect.

If a weapon, like some type of machine gun, has a fast fire rate, you can hold down the trigger and make it rain bullets on your enemy. How effective this is will depend on several factors, including the accuracy of your aim, the rarity of the weapon, the amount of ammo you have on hand for that weapon, and your distance from the opponent.

Floor/Ceiling Building Tile

This flat tile is one of the four shapes of building tiles you can use to create fortresses or structures, virtually anywhere on the island. Like all building tiles, these can be constructed from wood, stone, or metal, which determines how fast you can build, and the tile's HP strength (how much damage it'll take before being destroyed). In addition to using this type of tile to create floors or ceilings within structures or fortresses, you'll use it to build bridges, either for your soldier to walk across or to drive across with an ATK, for example.

Flush Factory

Found at map coordinates D9.5, this is an abandoned, multi-level toilet factory. Inside, explore the manufacturing area, as well as the offices and restrooms. There's plenty of useful loot to find and gather inside.

Inside the factory, build stairs or a ramp to reach the top of these restrooms, where you'll often discover a chest. Another chest can usually be found on the second level of the factory.

The building with the red ropes outside is a dance club. (Listen for the music coming from inside the building.) You can spend time dancing on the dance floor, but you'll be more productive if you search the area for loot.

If there are enemies lurking around, try to stay in the higher areas, so you can shoot at or defend against enemies from above them.

There's often a chest located behind the DJ booth that's located at the end of the dance floor, as well as in the office upstairs (if you use the stairs to the left when facing the DJ booth from the dance floor). Each of the other buildings in this area also offer useful weapons, ammo, loot, and occasionally chests. Be sure to check the trucks and metal containers found on the streets in this area.

Located near Flush Factory (near map coordinates E9) are a group of buildings that aren't labeled on the map.

Fortress

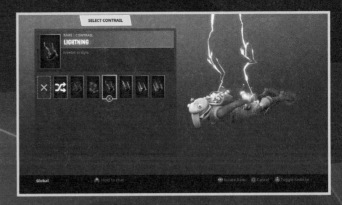

Using resources (wood, stone, and/or metal), you have the ability to build simple or extremely elaborate fortresses during a match in order to protect your soldier, or from which you can launch potentially devastating attacks, when you're armed with an explosive projectile weapon (such as a Rocket Launcher), or a long-range rifle (with or without a scope).

A simple fortress can be a single level, and include four walls around you, and maybe a roof. More elaborate fortresses can be many levels tall, and designed using your own creativity, based on the situation you're facing.

Freefall

As soon as you depart the Battle Bus, your soldier will freefall toward the ground. During this time, control the movement and falling speed of your soldier. This will help you reach a desired landing location.

Once you've acquired one or more contrail designs, select the one you want from the Locker prior to a match. From the Locker, select and highlight the Contrail option (located to the right of the Glider option), and then choose from an unlocked contrail.

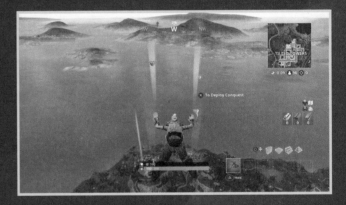

The contrail design you choose is seen during your soldier's freefall and is cosmetic only. It does not impact your soldier's rate of descent and offers zero tactical advantage.

Anytime during freefall, activate your soldier's glider to dramatically slow down their rate of descent and give you very precise control over their directional movements while traveling toward the ground. As your soldier is falling toward the island, you can activate and deactivate the glider as often as you wish. However, if you wait too long to deploy the glider, it will automatically activate as your soldier gets close to the ground—ensuring a safe landing.

G

Game Play Modes

The core *Fortnite: Battle Royale* game play modes include:

- **Solo**—One player competes against up to 99 opponents.
- **Duo**—A player and one teammate compete against up to 98 opponents. You can play with a friend or be matched up with a stranger by the game.
- **Squads**—A team of up to four players compete against all other opponents (out of a total of 100 players per match). You can play with friends or be matched up with up to three strangers by the game.
- **50 v 50** and **Playground** are two examples of temporary game play modes that are sometimes offered from the Choose Game Mode menu screen.

Game Update (Patch)

Every week or two weeks, Epic Games releases a game update (also referred to as a "patch.") You'll need to install the latest update of *Fortnite: Battle Royale* onto your gaming system before you can play.

Gaming Headset (with Microphone)

Sound is an extremely important element of the *Fortnite: Battle Royale* game play experience. It's essential that you be able to hear the sounds made by your opponents and be able to determine when your soldier is making too much noise as a result of his or her actions.

The best way to experience the audio incorporated into the game, and to be able to communicate verbally with your squad members (if applicable) is to use a gaming headset anytime you're playing *Fortnite: Battle Royale*. Shown here is a popular headset from Turtle Beach Corp. (www.turtlebeach.com), although many companies make stereo headsets with a built-in microphone that are compatible with all of the popular gaming platforms.

Glider

The glider is the device that's used to end a soldier's freefall and help him/her land safely on the island, while giving you precise control over your soldier's landing location. During freefall, you're able to activate and deactivate the glider as often as you like, but it automatically deploys during the final moments of freefall.

Just as many different and optional outfits are available for soldiers, many optional glider designs are available. Some can be purchased from the Item Shop, while others can be unlocked by completing challenges, for example. Once you've unlocked multiple glider designs, choose the one you want to use before any match by accessing the Locker. Each of the glider designs looks different, but they all work exactly the same way. The difference between glider designs is only their appearance.

Golf

One type of emote that can be unlocked is the golf ball. Add the golf ball to your Emotes menu from the Locker before a match. Then during the match, you're able to use your soldier's pickaxe as a golf club and select the golf ball to hit while on the golf course.

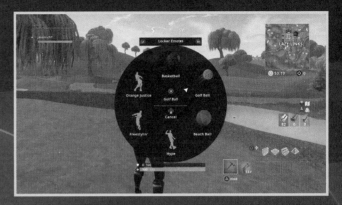

To play golf, find a place to stand on the golf course, in front of one of the holes. The holes have a flag associated with them. Select the golf ball from the Emotes menu.

Your soldier will swing their pickaxe, like a golf club, and send the ball forwards. Your job is to try to get a hole in one. There's no benefit to doing this other than to take a break from the fighting and to have fun. If you're playing a Duos or Squads game, you can challenge your partner or squad mates to a round of golf. Keep in mind, when playing golf, your soldier will be out in the open, and could become vulnerable to attack, so be prepared to defend yourself.

Graphic Emote

This is one of three types of emotes available. Refer to the listing for "Emotes," for more information. When a graphic emote is used, a soldier throws a graphic icon into the air for everyone in the immediate area to see. Each icon must be unlocked or acquired separately. Choose which graphic emotes you want accessible from the Locker.

During a match (or while in the pre-deployment area), access the Emotes menu to display a desired emote.

Grappler

A Grappler is a gun-shaped loot item that can be shot at a structure. When the suction cup end hits its target, your soldier is immediately and quickly drawn to the target location. Use this item to quickly reach the top of a building or to swing from structure to structure.

Greasy Grove

Fast food restaurants, plus a few stores, and several homes are what you'll encounter in this region of the island, which can be found at map coordinates C7.

The fast food restaurant has multiple levels, including a basement. Here you'll find a bunch of weapons, ammo, loot items, and resources. Be sure to explore the other buildings in this area to find loot and potentially hide from enemies. You can also place Traps or Remote Explosives within the buildings to surprise enemies with a painful blast. If you don't yet have a Trap, one might be for sale from a nearby Vending Machine.

Grenade Launcher

This is one of the more powerful projectile and explosive weapons available. From a distance, you can accurately aim at a target and fire this weapon. Upon impact, it'll explode. A direct hit to a building or structure will cause serious damage or result in it collapsing. A direct hit to an enemy soldier will usually cause their immediate demise. Most gamers save their Grenade Launcher until the End Game portion of a match, but this weapon can be used anytime to damage or pummel any structure, building, or enemy.

Grenades

These are weapons that get tossed at an enemy or target location. They explode on impact. The closer an enemy is to the explosion, the more damage it will cause. Grenades can also be used to destroy buildings or structures. A soldier can collect and carry multiple Grenades within a single backpack slot.

Toss one or two Grenades into a wooden structure, and it'll be destroyed in seconds. However, if your own soldier is too close to the explosion once a Grenade has been tossed, the damage could be devastating! Keep in mind, a Grenade can bounce off of a wall or object, and repel back toward the thrower, so be careful.

Guided Missile Launcher

This is one of the more powerful, long-range, explosive weapons available. It uses Rockets for ammo. Once you have one of these weapons, select it and aim at your target.

When you pull the trigger, you'll see the missile flying toward the target. While the missile is in midair, use the directional controls on your controller to navigate where the missile travels.

As soon as the missile from the Guided Missile Launcher hits its target, it'll explode. Use this type of weapon to destroy buildings or structures, and to injure or defeat anyone within them.

H

Haunted Hills

The churches, crypts, and a graveyard are what you'll find in this relatively small region (located at map coordinates B2.5). There's also great scavenging to be done here for chests, weapons, ammo, loot, and stone.

At the start of Season 6, a giant stone castle was added to the top of a mountain in this area of the island. The castle contains many rooms and chambers to explore.

Inside the churches, smash through the stone walls (and floor) to reveal hidden crypts and rooms that typically contain a chest, or at the very least, a weapon, as well as some ammo, or one or more loot items.

Inside the smaller stone crypts, you'll often discover loot items. These also provide a temporary shelter from enemy gunfire if you go inside and block the entrance by building a wall.

Be sure to explore the basement and tower within the church.

The church typically contains at least one or two chests. From the higher levels of a church, choose a sniping location, crouch down (to achieve better aim), and then use a shotgun, long-range rifle, or sniper rifle (with a scope) to target enemy soldiers below.

Health Points (HP)

Displayed near the bottom-center of the screen (on most gaming platforms) is a soldier's Health meter (displayed in green). The Shield meter is displayed directly above the Health meter (in blue). The Health meter displays the number of Health Points (HP) your soldier has remaining. This can be between zero and 100. When the Health meter (or the number of Health Points possessed) reaches zero, your soldier is immediately eliminated from the match.

Each time your soldier receives an injury, some of his or her HP gets depleted. This can be from a bullet wound, a fall, or the result of an explosion, for example.

Throughout a match, there are multiple ways to boost your soldier's HP. For example, you can consume an Apple, Chug Jug, or Slurp Juice. You can also utilize a Cozy Campfire, Bandages, or Med Kit.

All objects on the island, such as building tiles, ATK vehicles, and even trees, each have an HP meter associated with it. When enough damage is caused on that object, it'll be destroyed.

Heavy Bullets

This is the type of ammunition used by sniper rifles and other high caliber weapons that are designed for long-range shooting. As you collect ammo, it gets stored within your backpack. Check your Backpack Inventory screen to see how much of each type of ammo you have on hand at any given time.

I

Impulse Grenades

This type of grenade inflicts damage to enemies, plus throws them into the air, away from the point of impact. A soldier can collect and carry multiple Impulse Grenades in a single backpack slot. This type of weapon gets tossed at an enemy.

Island

The island is where every match takes place. On the island are more than 20 different (labeled) points of interest, in addition to an ever-growing number of areas that are not labeled on the map. Throughout a match, a soldier can travel anywhere on the map. However, it's best to avoid the deadly storm that forms and expands throughout the island once a match begins.

Island Map

While in the pre-deployment area, during freefall, or anytime while on the island, access the island map.

This is what the island map looked like during Season 6. Many of the island's points of interest are clearly labeled, although some smaller locations are not labeled. These unlabeled areas often offer multiple chests and an abundance of weapons, ammo, and loot items to find and collect. To make it easier to identify specific locations on the map, whether or not they're labeled, map coordinates are used.

Item Shop

Every day, a new selection of limited edition items, including outfits, pickaxe designs, glider designs, and emotes are available for purchase from the Item Shop. It's accessible from the Lobby. One item can be purchased at a time using V-Bucks (which cost real money to acquire).

limited edition. Outfits in other categories, such as "Epic" outfits, as well as "Rare" or "uncommon" outfits, get re-introduced every few weeks or months and are less expensive. This Diecast outfit is about to be purchased for 1,200 V-Bucks. It's classified as "Rare."

J

Jetpack

This is a limited-time loot item that periodically gets re-introduced into the game. If you find a Jetpack, strap it on, and for a short time, fly at a fast speed while controlling your soldier's movement. Use it to reach far off areas quickly, escape being caught in the storm, rush an opponent, or initiate an attack from midair.

Junk Junction

Found between map coordinates B1.5 and C1.5, old cars are piled up everywhere within Junk Junction. You'll often find items to collect on top of car piles. On the ground, between the piles, is a maze-like area to explore. This is just one of the junkyards on the island. Another can be found just outside of Paradise Palms.

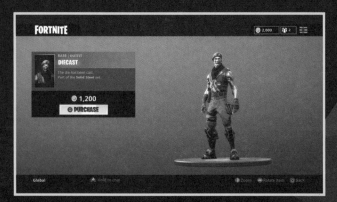

The items sold from the Item Shop that are classified as "Legendary" are typically only available for a single day and are considered

Outside of Junk Junction (near map coordinates B1), be sure to explore this llama-shaped tower to find several chests and other weapons.

As you can see here, the ground level of Junk Junction is a maze-like area. It's safer to explore Junk Junction from higher levels as opposed to ground level, especially if there are enemies lurking around. Either climb to the top of junk piles and jump between them or build bridges that'll help you stay on high ground.

Be sure to explore the buildings in the Junk Junction area, as well as the structures you'll discover just outside of Junk Junction.

If enemies have also found their way here, it's a good idea to defeat them first. Be sure to obtain a height advantage by climbing to the top of the car piles or the roof of a nearby building.

Use your soldier's pickaxe to smash the vehicles and harvest a ton of metal while you're in this area.

Located a short distance from Junk Junction (at map coordinates C1.5) is this warehouse that contains a movie set. Inside you'll stumble upon a few chests if you search carefully.

L

Landing Location

After departing from the Battle Bus and entering into freefall, this is the location on the island where you choose to land. Some players opt to land smack in the middle of a popular point of interest and are willing to confront enemy soldiers right from the start. Others choose to land in a more remote, less populated, or even deserted area of the island, which gives them more time to build up their arsenals and gather resources before having to engage in firefights or battle enemies.

Launch Pad

This item can be collected and used to quickly catapult your soldier into the air, activate his or her glider, and then precisely transport them to a different location. It is a rare item, but very useful for escaping the storm if you get stuck deep in uninhabitable territory. A Launch Pad is also useful to rush a distant opponent so you're able to quickly approach and launch a close-range attack.

To use a Launch Pad, it must be placed on a flat surface. Once it's placed on the ground, have your soldier step on the platform to activate it.

Your soldier will be catapulted into the air upon stepping on the Launch Pad. Once the soldier's glider deploys, steer it the same way as you did when your soldier first approached the island upon leaving the Battle Bus.

Lazy Links

This point of interest was added to the island at the start of Season 5. It's a country club with a golf course. The area contains a large clubhouse, a golf course, as well as several other structures. Because of its location, Lazy Links tends to be one of the more popular points of interest on the island, so you're virtually guaranteed to encounter enemies here.

This is one of the areas of the island where you'll find All Terrain Karts if you're one of the first soldiers to explore here during a match.

The swimming pool area almost always contains several chests. Check behind the counter, and then smash this wall to find a chest behind it.

Explore all of the smaller structures to see what you can find inside. In the structures that have a garage, sometimes you'll find an ATK inside. Other times, you'll discover a tractor inside. Smash the tractor to harvest metal.

The main country club building that overlooks the golf course contains multiple levels and many rooms. Almost all of them have stuff that's worth grabbing if you're the first soldier to explore here during a match.

Light Bullets

This type of ammunition is used with pistols, SMGs, and most handheld guns. It causes more damage when used at close range. To inflict the most damage, aim for a headshot or hit your target multiple times.

Lobby

This is the main screen from which you're able to choose a game play mode, enter into a match, view details about your soldier (including his/her experience level), see the current challenges, read bulletins from Epic Games, plus access the Battle Pass, Challenges, Locker, Item Shop, Career, and Store area, as well as the Settings menu.

Location Map

Continuously displayed on the screen during a match is a tiny Location Map. It's also referred to as the "mini map." Here it's shown in the top-right corner of the screen. Depending on which gaming system you're using, the location of this map will vary.

The Location Map shows your current position on the island using a white triangle icon. If you get caught in the storm, or you're outside of where the safe area will be once the storm expands, follow the white line to safety. If you're near the edge of the circle, the white line of the circle's perimeter is also displayed. Areas shown in pink are uninhabitable, due to the storm.

Locker

This is the virtual storage space where all of the character customization items you've purchased, unlocked, or acquired get stored when they're not being used. Access the Locker before a match to choose the appearance of your soldier using the items currently available to you.

The Locker is divided into three sections. On the right, your character's current appearance is displayed. Under the Account and Equipment heading, individual sections of the Locker allow you to choose your banner, outfit, back bling design, pickaxe design, contrail design, and loading screen design. Below these options, under the Emotes heading, choose six different types of emotes (including graphic emotes, dance moves, and spray paint tags) that you want to be able to utilize during a match.

Once you acquire a new item from the Item Shop or unlock a new item, it will appear automatically within the appropriate section of your Locker. If a small yellow banner displaying a number appears in the top-right corner of a Locker section, this means that new items are available. Only items that you've unlocked, acquired, or earned will be displayed within the Locker.

Lonely Lodge

Located at map coordinates J4.5, Lonely Lodge is where you'll find a camping lodge, a collection of cabins, parked RVs, and a tall observation tower.

The most exciting place to explore near this point of interest is this massive, waterfront mansion (found at map coordinates J5.5).

As you approach the front door of the mansion, use the pickaxe to smash into the ground. You'll discover the entrance to a hidden basement. It contains some type of high-tech base that's filled with awesome items to collect. There are several chests to be found here.

Within Lonely Lodge, be sure to explore the main lodge. You'll find chests and other goodies inside. It's the largest building in the area.

The tallest structure in the area is this wooden observation tower. Near the top in particular, you'll find some great weapons, loot items, and potentially several chests. If you climb to the top, don't fall or jump off, or you'll perish.

Many of the small cabins in the area contain weapons, ammo, and loot. You can easily booby trap one or more of these cabins with Traps or Remote Explosives. Another option is to hide inside one of the cabins, close the door behind you, crouch down, draw your weapon, and wait for an enemy soldier to enter. When they do, ambush them!

Loot Lake

In the middle of the lake (found at map coordinates E4), there's an island that contains a house. Inside, you'll discover chests and other useful items to collect. Then, make your way to the rowboat in the center of the lake, as well as the buildings (located near docks) on the opposite side of the lake.

If you attempt to reach the rowboat in the lake, empty the chest quickly, and be prepared to evade enemy fire. If you have a sniper rifle (or rifle with a scope), stay on land and shoot at enemy soldiers who attempt to reach the rowboat.

At the start of Season 6 the island in the middle of the lake started to float in midair and then move around. The lake itself now looks very different and the water in the center contains a massive whirlpool. The same structures can be found surrounding the lake, however.

Instead of walking through the lake to cross it (which is a slow process that leaves you out in the open and exposed to potential enemy attacks), build a wooden bridge over the water. You can walk across the bridge, or if you're driving an ATK, drive across it.

The house on the island is chock full of items worth collecting, so search carefully, but be prepared to encounter enemy soldiers.

The two warehouse buildings located near the docks are both worth searching, although you're more apt to find chests and useful loot in the larger of the buildings. As you approach either building, watch out for snipers.

Additional structures around Loot Lake include a wooden tower, a modern-looking house, and a small structure (with a dock in front of it). Most contain some awesomely useful loot. Consider traveling around the lake (instead

of crossing it) to explore the structures you encounter.

Loot Llama

While Supply Drops happen randomly throughout each match, they tend to be rare. An even rarer occurrence is finding a Loot Llama. This is a llama-shaped statue that looks like a colorful piñata. It contains a random collection of often rare loot, weapons, ammo, and/or resource icons (similar to a Supply Drop or chest).

Should you happen to stumble upon a Loot Llama, approach it with caution, in case enemies are nearby waiting to attack you. Consider quickly building four walls (and a ceiling) around you and the Loot Llama for protection before opening it.

Opening a Loot Llama takes about eight seconds. You then need time to safely pick and choose which items you want to grab. It'll often be necessary to take time to reorganize your backpack's inventory to accommodate the new, powerful, and rare weapons, ammo, and loot you find. This Loot Llama offered large bundles of wood and metal, along with a Launch Pad, Grenades, a Cozy Campfire, and a selection of ammo.

Watch out for flashing lights when you spot a Loot Llama. Instead of opening a Loot Llama, some gamers transform it into a weapon by attaching Remote Explosives to it. Then, as soon as someone else approaches, the explosives get detonated, and the approaching soldier is terminated with a bang. If you see the flashing lights of a Remote Explosive, stay clear and don't approach.

If you find yourself with a good arsenal and you don't need anything else, consider setting your own trap when you encounter a Loot Llama by attaching Remote Explosives to it. Then hide somewhere nearby and wait for an enemy to approach. You can also use a sniper rifle, so from a distance you're able to snipe at enemies approaching a Loot Llama.

Loot Items

One of the more important decisions you'll need to make during a match is choosing which type(s) of loot you want to carry in your backpack at any given time, so those items will be readily available to you. Remember, you only have six backpack slots, and one of those is always taken by your pickaxe. At least one or two of the remaining slots should be used to carry weapons, such as some type of gun.

Within a single backpack slot, you can hold multiples of the same loot items. For example, you can carry a bunch of Grenades, and then use them one at a time when they're needed. Some loot items, like Traps, Bouncer Pads, and Cozy Campfires get stored with your resources and don't require a slot within your backpack.

There are many types of loot items to be found and collected while visiting the island. The following chart shows you information about the various loot items that can be used to boost or replenish your soldier's Health and/or Shield meters. Other types of loot items can be used as tools, or as weapons, for example.

LOOT ITEM NAME	DESCRIPTION	REPLENISHES HEALTH	REPLENISHES SHIELDS	TIME REQUIRED TO USE OR CONSUME IT
Apples	Grab and consume an Apple right when and where you find it. It will replenish 5 points to your soldier's Health meter.	Yes	No	Almost Instant
Bandages	Boost your soldier's Health meter by 15 points each time you use Bandages.	Yes	No	4 Seconds
Chug Jug	Replenish your soldier's Health meter and Shield meter to 100.	Yes	Yes	15 Seconds
Cozy Campfire	For each second a soldier stands next to the flame, his or her health will increase by 2 points. The flame lasts 25 seconds.	Yes	No	25 Seconds
Med Kit	Replenish your soldier's Health meter back to 100.	Yes	No	10 Seconds
Mushrooms	Replenish your soldier's Shield meter by 5 points	No	Yes	Almost Instant
Shield Potion	Replenish your soldier's Shield meter by 50 points	No	Yes	5 Seconds
Slurp Juice	Replenish your soldier's Health meter *and* Shield meter by 25 points.	Yes	Yes	2 Seconds to Consume, and then up to 25 Seconds to Fully Utilize
Small Shield Potion	Replenish your soldier's Shield meter by 25 points.	No	Yes	2 Seconds

Lucky Landing

Found between map coordinates F10 and G10, the buildings in and around this point of interest all have an Asian influence. Within the building that contains the giant pink tree, you're apt to find rare and powerful weapons. However, be sure to explore all of the buildings, bridges, and towers in this region.

There are multiple chests to be found in the main rooms of the Asian temple, as well as most of the other buildings and structures you'll encounter in this area.

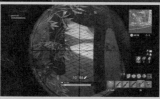

Go to the top floor of this office building. In addition to finding items within the building, the large window on the top floor offers a great view of the area, from which you can use any long-range weapon to shoot at enemy soldiers below.

Targeting enemies on the ground is easier with a rifle that contains a scope, but any rifle or shotgun should do the trick. As always, a headshot causes much more damage than a body shot. Using a projectile explosive, such as a Rocket Launcher, Guided Missile Launcher, or Grenade Launcher will destroy the structure you shoot at, and likely defeat anyone inside.

Don't forget to look inside the buildings, including behind the counters in stores and restaurants, to find chests. Check the shelves for ammo boxes. On the floor of almost every building in this area you'll discover weapons, ammo, or loot items waiting to be grabbed.

In the building with the pink tree in the center, weapons can often be found on the ground in every corner of the structure if you're the first person to get there. Smash the pink tree, and you'll often (but not always) discover a chest.

M

MAG (Magazine) Capacity

When it comes to evaluating the power and capabilities of a weapon, MAG Capacity represents the total number of ammunition rounds (or bullets) the weapon can hold at once, before it needs to be reloaded. Reloading a weapon takes valuable time, during which your soldier will be vulnerable to attack.

Shotguns have a small MAG Capacity but each round of ammunition packs a wallop when you make a direct hit. Machine guns and certain other weapons have a much larger MAG Capacity, but each individual bullet typically causes less damage when a direct hit is made.

Map Coordinates

The island map is divided into quadrants (boxes). Displayed along the top margin of the map (from left to right) are the letters "A" through "J." Along the left margin of the map, from top to bottom, are the numbers "1" through "10." Using these letters and numbers, you can easily identify any location or quadrant on the map.

While viewing the island map, it's possible to zoom in and scroll around in order to view a particular area of the island in more detail. By zooming in on areas of the map, you can more closely see unlabeled points of interest.

Match

A match begins the moment up to 100 soldiers land on the island and ends when only one soldier remains alive and most of the island has become uninhabitable due to the expansion of the storm. The average match lasts about 15 minutes, but its duration has a lot to do with the skill of the players, and how quickly eliminations happen.

Med Kits

Whether it's the result of a gunshot wound, getting caught in an explosion, spending time in the storm, or taking a fall, it's extremely likely that during a match, your soldier will take damage, and at least some of the Health Points (HP) from their Health meter will be depleted.

Consuming a Med Kit restores your health to 100 percent. It takes 10 seconds to use a Med Kit, during which time your soldier is vulnerable to attack.

Med Kits can be found in chests and Supply Drops, acquired from Vending Machines, or after defeating an enemy and taking their loot. Occasionally, you'll spot a Med Kit lying on the ground waiting to be collected. Within your backpack, you're able to store multiple Med Kits in a single slot, and then use them, one at a time, when they're needed.

Medium Bullets

This type of ammo is used within assault rifles and similar weapons. It's ideal for mid-range shooting, although the closer you are to your target, the more damage each bullet will inflict.

Metal

Metal is one of the three types of resources you'll need to collect or harvest during a match. When it comes to building, metal is the strongest material available to you. It can withstand the most damage before it's destroyed. As a result, building a protective wall or fort from metal gives you the most protection.

Metal can be harvested using your pickaxe to smash anything made of metal that you discover on the island. This includes cars, trucks, metal fencing, farm silos, machinery, or kitchen appliances found in homes, for example. Anytime you harvest metal, it makes a lot of noise and can easily attract enemy soldiers to your location.

Additional ways to collect metal include defeating enemy soldiers and collecting their resources or finding and grabbing metal icons (shown here) that are scattered throughout the island. Resource icons can sometimes be found within chests, Supply Drops, or Loot Llamas too.

Miniguns

This is just one of the many types of weapons to be found, collected, and used on the island. Miniguns can be used from any range and are useful for spraying a wall or structure with bullets in order to destroy it. Of course, this type of weapon can cause some major damage when a bunch of bullets from it hit an enemy soldier.

Muscle Memory

The concept of establishing and using your muscle memory applies when playing almost any computer or video game. The goal is to practice playing, and repeat the same actions so often, that they become second nature to you. In other words, you train yourself to know exactly what to press on the wireless controller, keyboard/mouse, or touchscreen, and know exactly when to do it, so you don't need to waste time thinking about it.

In terms of playing *Fortnite: Battle Royale*, with practice, you'll want to train your muscle memory to help you accomplish common tasks, including:

- Quickly switching between and selecting weapons within your backpack.
- Aiming your selected weapon and firing accurately at your targets.
- Switching between building, resource collection/harvesting, and fighting mode.
- Quickly building structures and being able to switch between building pieces and building materials.
- Accessing the island map, Emotes menu, and Quick Chat menu during a match.

Motel

You won't see this labeled on the island map, but located between map coordinates D2 and E2, you'll discover this rundown motel. This is one of the structures of the structures in this area, it includes several former guestrooms that contain multiple items to collect.

Mushrooms

You'll find blue Mushrooms randomly lying on the ground, often under trees or in swampy areas. When you pick up a Mushroom and consume it, your soldier's Shield meter increases by 5 points. This item must be consumed when and where it's found. It can't be picked up and stored within your soldier's backpack for future use.

N

Nerfed

This is a term used by gamers when describing how a weapon or loot item's power, strength, or capabilities within *Fortnite: Battle Royale* have been reduced as the result of Epic Games tweaking some aspect of the game in conjunction with a game patch (update). For example, in a game patch released in July 2018, Epic Games "nerfed" the HP strength of wood

tiles, meaning that structures or fortresses you build out of wood can now withstand less damage before getting destroyed.

O

Outfits

Every day Epic Games releases new outfits you can purchase for your soldier. Throughout this guide, many different (optional) outfits and soldier customizations are shown.

Outfits are available from the Item Shop. In addition, you're able to unlock outfits by accomplishing Battle Pass–related goals or by acquiring free downloadable items from promotional partners. (See the listing or "Twitch Prime Packs.")

P

Paradise Palms

At the start of Season 5, an entire region of the map was transformed into a desert area. In the heart of this region is Paradise Palms, a small city that contains a bunch of multi-story buildings, along with a small community of single-family homes.

The tallest building in Paradise Palms is this hotel. Within it, you'll discover many rooms that contain chests, loot items, weapons, and ammo. Outside the hotel is a swimming pool area that's often chock full of useful things to grab. Parked outside of the hotel, you'll often find an ATK, if you're one of the first people to reach this area.

Paradise Palms has become one of the most popular points of interest on the island, so expect to encounter multiple enemies here. Explore each of the buildings, homes, and structures, and use them to your advantage when launching attacks. In and around Paradise Palms, you'll often discover Rifts.

Patch Notes

Every time Epic Games releases a game update for *Fortnite: Battle Royale* on its website you'll find an "Announcements" and "Patch Notes" section. These sections of the website explain what's new and what's been tweaked or changed within the game.

To read the latest Patch Notes, visit: www.epicgames.com/fortnite/en-US/news.

If you land on the roof of this hotel, or travel up to the roof, your soldier can look out and see much of the region, plus have a height advantage, which makes it easier to shoot at enemies below.

Pets

Of one the cutest additions ever made to *Fortnite: Battle Royale* was virtual pets that a soldier can carry around in their backpack. While these pets are somewhat interactive, they do not offer any tactical advantage.

A virtual pet can only be unlocked by completing challenges associated with a Battle Pass. At the start of Season 6, when you completed Tier #12, it unlocked a virtual dog. Completing Tier #29 unlocked a lizard-like creature.

Each virtual pet comes with their own back bling that your soldier wears. Any of the virtual pets can be linked with any outfit. This adorable dragon becomes available from the Back Bling section of the Locker when you unlock Tier #43 during Season 6.

Pickaxe

The pickaxe is a soldier's primary tool. It's available from the moment a soldier steps foot on the island, and when it's not in use, it gets stored within a soldier's backpack. It can't be dropped or replaced.

Use the pickaxe to harvest resources, smash apart or break through objects, and as a close-range weapon. Almost every outfit that Epic Games releases has an optional and matching pickaxe design. All pickaxes work exactly the same way.

From the Locker, you're able to choose the appearance of your pickaxe based on the designs you've purchased, unlocked, or acquired.

Pistols

There are many types of handheld pistols available on the island. These tend to be common and useful close-range weapons. They are far less powerful and less versatile, however, than other types of weapons, such as shotguns.

Early in a match, grab a pistol and make it part of your arsenal, but this should be one of the first items to replace in your full backpack, when more powerful weapons (that can also be used for close-range combat) become available. If you have a choice between a single pistol or Duel Pistols, go with the Duel Pistols and take advantage of the extra fire power.

Pleasant Park

In addition to Snobby Shores, this is an area of the island that contains a bunch of single-family homes. Found at map coordinates C3, there's also a park and sports field within this point of interest.

The structure in the center of town often contains a chest, as well as a centralized location from which you can shoot at enemies in all directions around you. Build a mini-fort above the structure in the center of town, and you'll have a 360-degree view of the area. Using a shotgun, sniper rifle, or any rifle with a scope, you'll be able to pick off enemy soldiers with relative ease, without having to move around too much.

Inside the homes, you may encounter enemy soldiers, so listen carefully for their footsteps and movements, especially before you open the door to a room or climb up or down stairs. Explore these single-family homes just as you would any other homes on the island, paying extra attention to the attic, basement, or garage if you're looking for chests.

Point of Interest

A point of interest is a location on the island map that is labeled, and that tends to be popular. Each point of interest features a different type of terrain, offers a different selection of buildings and structures to explore, and contains an assortment of chests, weapons, ammo, loot, and resources that can be collected.

The island map contains approximately twenty points of interest that are labeled on the map, along with several areas that are smaller and not labeled.

As each new gaming season kicks off, you'll discover alterations to the island map. For example, you might discover a new point of interest, or notice that a point of interest has been dramatically altered.

Keep in mind, anytime a new point of interest is added to the island map, it becomes an extremely popular landing spot, because everyone wants to check it out. As a result, as soon as you land there, you'll typically encounter many enemy soldiers. To survive, you must be one of the first to land, and then find and grab a weapon. Otherwise, you'll get shot within moments after landing, while you're still unarmed.

When you want to visit a very popular point of interest, consider landing in the outskirts of that area. Collect weapons, ammo, loot items, and resources first, and then go into that area fully armed and ready to fight. While you'll likely survive longer, you'll notice that as a latecomer to the area during a match, the chests are likely to have been opened, and the available weapons, ammo, and loot items will

have been collected. By defeating enemies, however, you can grab everything they've collected.

The first few times you visit a new and popular point of interest, take the time to discover the location of chests, as well as where other weapons and items will likely be found in the future. Once you get to know the area, when you return in future matches, you'll know exactly where to go to find the best loot items, and where to go to stay safe.

Port-A-Fort

This is a loot item that's rare. Once found, however, it can be picked up and carried within your backpack until it's needed. When activated, a multi-level metal fort is instantly built. This fortress requires no resources to build.

Use a Port-A-Fort to protect yourself from an incoming attack, or for additional protection as you use long-range or projectile weapons to launch an attack on others. Inside the fort are tires you can bounce on in order to reach the top of the fort quickly. From the top, if you look out over the edge, you'll get a 360-degree view of the surrounding area. Move down a bit, but stay near the top (shown), and your soldier will be protected.

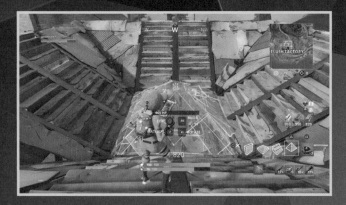

To ensure that an enemy does not follow you into a Port-A-Fort, as soon as you enter and reach the top of it, immediately build a flat floor/ceiling tile to fill in the opening. This will slow down an enemy. For added protection, build a metal pyramid-shaped tile on top of the floor tile. Another option is to place a Cozy Fireplace on top of the floor tile, so you can replenish some of your soldier's Health meter while hiding out within the fortress. A Port-A-Fortress is like a Port-A-Fort, but rarer. When built, it becomes a much larger structures that's well fortified.

Pre-Deployment Area

Prior to boarding the Battle Bus, this is the holding area where you'll wait until all of the players have joined the match. Any weapons or resources you find and collect in this area will be taken away when you board the Battle Bus. Feel free to explore this area, practice your dance moves, and try using your other emotes, for example. You can't be harmed in the pre-deployment area, so don't worry about being shot at or getting whacked by an enemy's pickaxe.

Pyramid-Shaped Building Tile

This is one of the four shaped building tiles available to you when in Building mode. These can be used on the roof of a structure to provide yourself with additional safe places to crouch behind, for example.

If you need quick protection on ground level, consider building a few metal pyramid-shaped tiles, and then crouching down behind them.

Especially when building with metal, it takes time for a building tile to complete. While the building process is taking place, a tile's HP slowly increases, until it's fully built. As a result, it won't offer full protection during the building process.

Meanwhile, if a tile receives damage from an enemy's weapon, you can stick around and repair the damage (which requires resources) or leave the structure before it gets destroyed.

Q

Quick Builder Controller Layout

This particular controller layout makes the commonly used game features associated with building more readily accessible. If you're a noob, initially stick with the Old School ("Standard") controller layout, because it makes the commonly used features for fighting, resource gathering, and building all easily accessible.

Once you gain experience playing *Fortnite: Battle Royale*, and you discover your personal strategy focuses heavily on building, then consider switching to the Quick Builder or Pro Builder controller layout.

R

Racetrack

Found in the desert area of the island (between map coordinates I6.5 and J6.5) is this racetrack that's surrounded by several buildings. It's here you're guaranteed to find multiple All Terrain Karts if you're among the first soldiers to visit. Inside and surrounding the buildings (and the racetrack itself), you'll also discover an abundance of chests, weapons, ammo, loot items, and resource icons.

After hopping into the driver's seat of an ATK, pull up to the starting line on the racetrack, and when the lights turn green start racing around the track. How long it takes you to make successful laps around the track will be timed. As you're exploring or driving around the racetrack, watch out for enemy soldiers looking to attack your vehicle.

An ATK can easily be attacked using any type of gun or explosive weapon. A direct hit from a Rocket Launcher, Guided Missile Launcher, or Grenade Launcher will destroy an ATK and defeat whoever is riding inside. If you're close to the moving ATK, tossing a few Grenades or Clingers at it will also cause major damage.

Ramp/Stairs Building Tile

This is one of the more versatile building tiles available to you. It can be used to build ramps so you can reach otherwise inaccessible areas, or used to create ramps that'll give you a height advantage over your opponents. When you build this tile from wood, a ramp is created. When you build the same tile from stone or metal, stairs with a higher HP are created.

Reload Time

All of the different types of guns have a MAG Capacity that determines how many bullets (or how much ammo) the weapon can hold. Once you use this ammo, assuming you have collected additional ammo, you'll need to reload the weapon. The reload time determines how long it takes to reload an empty weapon.

During the reload time, you can't shoot, and you're basically defenseless. Seriously consider hiding behind an object for added protection while reloading. Weapons with a slow reload time tend to use the most powerful bullets or ammo. Thus, one direct hit will cause a lot of damage. However, if your aim isn't too good, each round of ammo you use will result in little or no damage to your enemy. Then, when it comes time to reload, you'll be vulnerable to an incoming attack.

Until you've become a pro at aiming weapons, stick with weapon choices that have a large MAG capacity and a quick reload time. Then, once you've perfected your aiming skills, consider using a weapon with more powerful ammo, but that has a slower reload time. One or two direct hits or headshots from a weapon with a slow reload time will defeat an enemy, so the reload time won't be an issue.

Remote Explosives

A soldier can carry up to 10 of these explosives at once. Activate it by attaching it to an object, wall, or structure, for example, and then detonate it remotely from any distance away.

After setting up a Remote Explosive, lure your adversary to its location before detonating it. Just make sure your soldier is far enough away to avoid the explosion. Watch for the blue light to know it's active.

Resources

Wood, stone, and metal are the three resources you'll want to collect and utilize during each match. Resources can be used for building, but they can also be used to purchase items from Vending Machines.

Scattered throughout the island are Wood, Stone, or Metal icons. Grab these to collect a bundle of that resource. Also, anytime you defeat an enemy soldier during a match, in addition to collecting their weapons, ammo, and loot items, you can also grab their resources.

As you prepare for the End Game portion of a match, when you may need to build at least one tall and sturdy fort or a series of ramps, you'll ideally want to have up to 1,000 wood, stone, and/or metal resources at your disposal. The more resources you have, the better.

Retail Row

Found at map coordinates H5.5, this area contains a handful of shops, restaurants, a water tower, plus a few homes, most of which surround street parking areas. One of the unique things about this region is that chests are not always found in the same place.

You'll often discover a chest at the top of the water tower.

From the roof of this home, located near the end of Retail Row, smash your way downward. This home is missing a piece of its roof. If you look carefully, you'll spot a chest from above. If you know an enemy is hiding within a house or structure and you have explosive weapons at your disposal (such as a Grenade Launcher or Remote Explosive), blow up or destroy that house or structure. The enemy will likely perish.

Most of the stores and restaurants have weapons, ammo, and loot items lying out in the open, on the ground, waiting to be collected. However, look for hidden rooms and areas where additional items, including chests, may also be available.

Revive (Heal)

When playing a Duos, Squads, or 50 v 50 match, your soldier has the ability to Revive (or heal) a partner, squad mate, or team member who has been injured. If you're able to reach an injured soldier before their Health meter is depleted, walk up to them and press the Revive button on your controller (keyboard/ mouse). It takes time to heal someone, during which time both your soldier and the soldier you're healing are vulnerable to attack. Make sure you're both in a safe area before attempting to Revive someone.

Rifts

You'll randomly encounter Rifts on the island, especially in the desert area. If you walk or drive an ATK into a Rift, your soldier will be catapulted into the air. Use your directional controls to navigate as they land. A Rift allows you to travel a decent distance quickly. Use them to outrun the storm, for example. After Season 5, however, Rifts may be vaulted and become a thing of the past.

Rifts-to-Go

While Rifts are a random phenomenon, Rifts-to-Go are a separate loot item that your soldier can find and carry in his or her backpack until it's needed. Once activated, the soldier gets catapulted into the air. Use the navigational controls on your controller (or keyboard/mouse) to guide the soldier to a desired landing location as he descends back to land with the help of a Glider. Use a Rift-to-Go to help you evade the storm, to escape from a battle, to leap from a tall building or structure (without getting injured), or to quickly travel to another location. When your soldier lands, he or she will not be injured from the fall.

Risky Reels

Found at map coordinates H2, Risky Reels includes a drive-in movie theater. In the parking lot are a bunch of abandoned cars and trucks that you can hide behind during a firefight or smash with your pickaxe in order to collect metal.

Check the backs of trucks for chests and loot items, and then explore the area near the movie screen, as well as the nearby buildings.

Within the large shed containing picnic tables, you'll often find at least one chest, as well as other weapons and loot items lying out in the open.

Rock Formations

Scattered throughout the island are rock formations. Hide behind large rock formations for protection. Using your pickaxe, smash apart the rocks to harvest stone.

Rocket Launcher

Use a Rocket Launcher as a long-range and explosive projectile weapon to destroy buildings and structures (and defeat anyone who's

hiding within them). One direct hit from a Rocket Launcher will defeat any enemy, regardless of how far away they are.

Rockets Ammo

This is the ammo used by Rocket Launchers, Grenade Launchers, and Guided Missile Launchers. Even if you don't yet have one of these powerful projectile weapons, collect as much Rockets ammo as you can throughout the match. Then, when you do add a compatible weapon to your arsenal, you'll be able to take many shots with it. This type of explosive ammo can be used to utterly destroy buildings and structures from a distance, so it's extremely useful during the End Game.

Roof Landing

Since the best weapons, ammo, and loot can often be found in the attics of homes and mansions, as well as on the top level of towers, buildings, and other tall structures (like silos, clock towers, and water towers), consider landing on the roof of a house, building, or structure after exiting the Battle Bus. Then, from the roof, use your pickaxe to smash your way downward.

As you're about to land on a roof, if you notice an enemy soldier has already landed there, you have three choices. First, you can land near the enemy and use your pickaxe to attack them. Victory will require multiple direct hits. Second, if you see a weapon nearby, be the first to grab it, and then shoot the other soldier (before he has a chance to grab that weapon). Third, choose an alternate landing site.

When you land on a roof, knowing that there's a chest in the attic or top floor directly below, you'll need to smash through the roof to reach it. If another soldier chooses to land on the same roof, the soldier who breaks through the roof, reaches the chest, and grabs the first weapon will likely shoot and defeat the other.

Run

In addition to walking and tiptoeing, running is one of the main ways your soldier can move around on the island. It also tends to be the fastest, unless you happen to have an ATK, Shopping Cart, Launch Pad, Bouncer Pad, or Jetpack at your disposal.

To keep running, press and hold down the Run button on your controller (or mouse/keyboard). There's also an optional Run Lock option, so your soldier will keep running, without you having to hold down the Run button.

Rush Opponent

Rushing an opponent means you quickly move toward them to launch a close-range attack. For example, during the End Game portion of a match, if you and an adversary are both safe within your respective fortresses, and you decide to leave your fortress and run toward the enemy fortress to attack it, this is referred to as rushing your opponent. It's also referred to as "pushing" your enemy.

S

Salty Springs

Found at map coordinates F7, here you'll discover a group of single-family homes and a gas station that are clustered together. Be sure to search the homes, but be on the lookout for enemy soldiers who may be lurking within them.

As always, if you're about to search a home, mansion, or building, and you notice the front or back door is already open, this means someone else has gotten there before you (possibly multiple people) and they could still be inside.

The homes in Salty Springs and throughout the island may all look different from the outside, but inside, most contain several floors, each with a handful of rooms.

Seasons

Every three to four months, Epic Games introduces a new gaming season in _Fortnite: Battle Royale_. This includes a significant game update that typically introduces new weapons, loot items, points of interest, challenges, and a new Battle Pass. At the start of each new season, your soldier's Experience Level returns to 1, but you keep all of your outfits and related items that you've purchased or unlocked.

Settings Menu

Access the Settings menu to tweak a handful of game play features. Especially if you're new to playing _Fortnite: Battle Royale_, don't waste time tinkering with these options. As you become better acquainted with the game, consider making small adjustments to the features that you think will make you more competitive. For example, make sure Auto Equip Better Items, Aim Assist, Turbo Building, and Auto Material Change are turned on.

Turning on Auto Pick Up Weapons can save you valuable seconds when you come across new weapons that you want to grab. When turned on, you simply need to run over to a weapon to grab it. Keep in mind, if your backpack is full and your soldier grabs a new weapon, whichever weapon he/she was holding and that was selected will be dropped. The new one will be picked up automatically.

Shells (Ammo)

This type of ammo is used by shotguns. It will inflict the most damage at close range, but shotguns can be used when you're at any distance from your target. The farther you are away, the less damage each direct hit will inflict.

Shield Meter

Throughout each match, your Shield meter is displayed as a blue bar. Here, it can be seen near the bottom-center of the screen, above the Health meter. However, the location of the Health and Shield meters will vary, based on what gaming platform you're using.

Shield Potion

This is one of the loot item powerups you can find, acquire, and consume during a match. Within a single slot of your backpack, it's possible to store multiple Shield Potions, and then consume them, one at a time, as you deem necessary. Like all loot items, Shield Potions can be found within chests, within Supply Drops or Loot Llamas, acquired from defeated enemies, or sometimes found lying on the ground (out in the open).

Each time you drink a Shield Potion, your shield meter increases by 50 (up to a maximum of 100). Drink two in a row to fully activate and replenish your soldier's shields. This item takes several seconds to consume, during which time your soldier is vulnerable to attack.

Shields

In addition to Health Points, one of the things that can help keep you alive during a match are shields. Shields can protect your soldier against enemy attacks. However, shields will *not* protect against falls or damage caused by the storm. How much added protection you'll have will depend on the level of your Shield meter.

When you have active shields and your soldier receives damage, first his or her Shield meter will get depleted, based on the severity of the damage. Then, if additional damage is inflicted once the soldier's Shield meter reaches zero, his or her Health meter will be negatively impacted. Find and consume a Small Shield Potion, Shield Potion, Slurp Juice, Mushrooms, or a Chug Jug to activate or replenish your soldier's Shield meter.

Shifty Shafts

Found at map coordinates D7, in addition to the buildings and structures you can see above ground, this region contains a maze-like collection of underground mining tunnels.

You'll find chests, as well as weapons, ammo, and loot on the ground within the mine tunnels. Crouch down and tiptoe your way through the mine tunnels, so enemies won't hear you approaching. As you approach a turn or intersection, have your weapon drawn and be ready to encounter an enemy soldier who's also exploring this region.

Shockwave Grenade

This is another loot item that can be found, collected, stored in your soldier's backpack, and then used anytime it's convenient. You can use this item to send yourself, your allies, or your enemies flying into the air like a cannonball.

No matter how high up a soldier goes when airborne, he'll always land safely without getting injured.

Shopping Carts

Scattered randomly throughout the island, mostly within points of interest, are Shopping Carts. Push one of these items up a hill or mountain, and then hop on it to ride down the hill. One soldier can push the Shopping Cart and another can ride within it when playing a Duos or Squads match, for example.

Between map coordinates B4.5 and C4.5 you'll discover a mountain. On the top of it are a handful of Shopping Carts and ramps jutting out in multiple directions. Grab a cart and take

Shotguns

Many gamers believe that any type of shotgun is the most versatile weapon offered on the island. There are several types to choose from (including Double Barrel Shotguns, Heavy Shotguns, Pump Shotguns, and Tactical Shotguns). These weapons are more powerful than a pistol, for example.

Shotguns can be used in close-range or mid-range combat situations, or even at a distance. (From a distance, they're harder to aim accurately than a rifle with a scope, for example.) When using a shotgun, always try for a headshot to inflict the most damage.

Slide Down Hills

Especially as you travel between points of interest on the island, you'll encounter hills and mountains. Surrounding many tall hills and mountains are steep cliffs. If you attempt to leap off of a cliff, you will either take damage (lose HP), or get injured so badly you'll be eliminated from the match.

Instead of jumping off a cliff, walk to the extreme edge, and then slide down it by pointing your directional controller inward. Sliding down even the steepest hill or cliff is safe. Keep in mind, you can't slide off ramps, stairs

Slurp Juice

As you drink each Slurp Juice, your soldier's Health *and* Shield meters increase by one point every second (for up to 25 seconds). While you're drinking, your soldier must be standing still and is vulnerable to attack.

Within a single slot of your backpack, you're able to carry around multiple Slurp Juices, that you can then consume, one at a time, as you need them. Your Health and Shield meters both max out at 100 points. If your Health meter is at 85 and your Shields are at 80, consuming a Slurp Juice will bring both meters back to 100, but not higher.

Small Shield Potion

A Small Shield Potion is less powerful than a Shield Potion. These are two separate types of items, and if you have one or more of each, they will require two slots within your backpack.

Consuming a Small Shield Potion increases your shield strength by 25 (up to a maximum of 100), but it takes several seconds to drink, during which time your soldier is vulnerable to attack.

SMGs (Submachine Guns)

This is another category of weapon available on the island. There are multiple variations of SMGs, which tend to offer a large MAG Capacity and can spew out many rounds of ammunition per second. The farther away you are from your target, the less accurate your aim will be and the less damage each bullet will cause.

SMGs are ideal for close-range to mid-range combat, but they work okay as long-range weapons too. They're particularly useful for shooting at and destroying ramps, structures, or walls.

Sniper Attack

Fortnite: Battle Royale includes several types of sniper rifles and rifles with scopes. These are superior for long-range attacks because you can aim them very precisely.

A sniper attack (using a rifle with a scope) works best when your soldier is safe behind some type of protective barrier and is both far away and higher up than the target. For improved accuracy, crouch down when aiming your weapon, use the scope, and pull the trigger when your target is centered within the crosshairs.

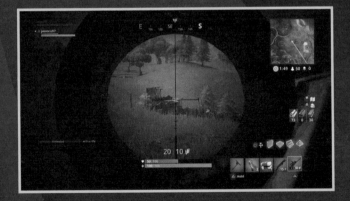

When you aim a rifle with a scope attached to it, you'll really be able to zoom in and target an opponent who is far away. Many gamers use the rifle's scope as binoculars to safely spy on far-away enemies.

Sniper Rifle (with Scope)

A sniper rifle is a rifle with a scope, so it can be used to accurately target enemies from a distance. A direct hit, especially a headshot, will be devastating to your opponent.

Take a moment to carefully aim your rifle when using a scope. A sniper rifle has a small MAG Capacity and slow Reload Time, so if your first one or two shots don't hit their target, take cover to avoid getting shot at while the weapon reloads.

Snobby Shores

Located at map coordinates A5, this is where the rich people who formally populated the island once lived. The area contains several lovely waterfront mansions, each of which offers multiple floors and many rooms to explore.

In addition to searching the mansions, be sure to search the security buildings and storage buildings located near many of the mansions. Also, don't forget to search the attics and basements (when applicable) of each mansion. This is typically where you'll discover chests.

Before entering any mansion or home, listen carefully for noises coming from inside. Also, peek through the windows and make sure the coast is clear. Don't forget, you can always surprise an enemy by shooting through a window. If you know someone is already inside, and you're not afraid to confront them, consider entering any mansion or home through the garage or backdoor, as opposed to the front door. Be unpredictable.

Solo Game Play Mode

Solo mode in *Fortnite: Battle Royale* means you must act alone on the island, as you attempt to outlive (and potentially defeat) up to 99 other opponents, without any assistance from a partner or squad. Choose the Solo game play mode from the Lobby before a match.

Sound FX Volume

By listening carefully to the sound effects in the game, you can often determine the location of enemies, and how close they are to you. Hearing all of the sound effects clearly will give you an advantage, so always pay attention to what you're hearing, as well as what you're seeing.

Sound effects play a crucial role in *Fortnite: Battle Royale*. For example, every soldier causes the sound of footsteps to be heard when they walk, run, or tiptoe. Smashing objects also makes noise, as do the sounds of explosions or weapon fire. Every time a door is opened or closed, everyone who is nearby will hear the squeak of the hinges.

From the Settings menu, choose the Audio submenu option, and then turn up the Sound FX Volume option to a level that allows you to hear everything.

Spectator Mode

Getting eliminated from a match can be a depressing and often frustrating experience. Instead of getting annoyed and immediately exiting back to the Lobby, stick around and stay in Spectator mode, so you can watch the rest of the match unfold.

Watching others, especially highly skilled and experienced gamers, play *Fortnite: Battle Royale* can be extremely useful for helping you develop your own game play strategies. Figure out what other players are doing right when it comes to fighting, building, and exploring, and try to mimic or improve upon their strategies in the future.

Spray Paint Tag Emotes

This is one of three types of emotes that your soldier can use throughout a match. A spray paint tag allows you to quickly paint a selected design onto any flat surface, such as a wall, tree, roof, or vehicle. During a match, access the Emotes menu, stand in front of the object you want to paint, and then select your tag design.

Squad Up

When playing the Squad game play mode, this is the process of inviting up to three of your friends to play with you on the same team.

If three friends aren't available, but you still want to play using the Squad mode, select the Fill option, and the game will match you up with additional players. When playing with one or more allies, communication during the match is essential. Either use a gaming headset so you can talk in real time or rely on using the Quick Chat menu.

Squads Game Play Mode

This is one of the permanent game play modes offered in *Fortnite: Battle Royale*. It allows you to team up with up to three friends or team members. You'll work together to defeat all of the enemy soldiers on the island, so you and/or one or more of your team members becomes the last person or people alive at the end of a match.

By selecting the Fill option after selecting the Squads game play mode, the game itself will match you up with three other (random) players. Throughout the match, the username, Health meter, and Shield meter for each team member is displayed in the top-left corner of the game screen. This may vary, based on what gaming platform you're using.

You can identify your team members by their appearance. Their username also appears directly over their heads. When you're not close to your team members, a message appears on the screen showing you what direction they're in. Plus, you can identify them on the Location Map that's displayed on the screen.

Stink Bombs

This weapon is just like a Grenade. It gets tossed at an enemy or within the vicinity of an enemy. When a Stink Bomb detonates, for 9 seconds a yellow stink cloud is created. For every half-second a soldier is stuck in the cloud, he or she loses 5 points from their Shield or Health meter.

Stone (also known as Brick)

Stone is one of the three types of resources you're able to collect and build with during a match. Stone is stronger than wood, but slower to build with. It is, however, weaker than metal (and faster to build with than metal).

Storage Depots

There are several cargo storage facilities on the island, including one found at map coordinates H4.5. They're not labeled on the map. Each of these areas contain many large cargo containers. The area somewhat resembles Junk Junction, in that there are piles of storage containers everywhere.

Inside the cargo containers, as well as above them, and within the neighboring buildings, you'll discover lots of useful items to collect, so you can expand your arsenal. The containers make great hiding spots, or you can booby trap them using Traps or Remote Explosives, for example, and then try to lure your enemies inside.

Your best bet, however, is to stay high up, so you can look and shoot downward at your enemies below. Be sure to check the buildings that surround the cargo containers. Inside, you're apt to discover chests and other goodies.

On ground level, the position of the containers creates a maze-like area you'll need to navigate through. Inside the containers, you'll often find great stuff to grab. The containers with two open ends can be used as a tunnel as you make your way through the maze on ground level. The containers with just one open door provide excellent shelter.

To quickly reach higher ground, build a ramp and get yourself to the top of the containers. Then once you're high up, shoot down at enemies who are still scampering around at ground level.

Storm

One of the challenges you'll encounter on the island is the deadly storm. As a match progresses, the storm expands and moves, taking up more and more of the island, and making more of the land uninhabitable. This forces the surviving soldiers to keep moving in order to stay within the safe area.

As long as your soldier has HP in their Health meter, he or she can stay within the storm ravaged areas for a short time. However, doing so will cause their Health meter to take a hit. During later stages of a match, the damage inflicted by staying in the storm-ravaged (unsafe) area increases, and damage happens faster. If you wind up staying within the storm for too long, you'll perish!

If you must enter into the storm, make sure your Health meter is maxed out in order to stay alive longer. The white triangle on the map shows your current location, and the white line shows the fastest and most direct route to follow in order to escape the storm.

Storm Rider (Storm Trooper)

Entering into the storm for a short amount of time will cause your soldier's Health meter to take a hit, but the exposure won't be lethal if you exit the storm before the Health meter reaches zero. For this reason, some gamers choose to hide in the storm for short periods of time or go into the storm to reposition themselves and launch a surprise attack on an enemy. When you use the storm to your tactical advantage you're referred to as a "Storm Rider" or "Storm Trooper."

Structures

There are many types of structures on the island. As you encounter each type, figure out how you can best utilize it to your advantage. Do you need a place to hide? Are you looking for a location that offers a tactical advantage from which to launch an attack? Do you need to locate weapons, ammo, or loot items to expand your arsenal?

Using any type of explosive weapons, such as Grenades, Remote Explosives, or a projectile explosive weapon (such as a Rocket Launcher, Guided Missile Launcher, or Grenade Launcher), any pre-built or soldier-built structure can be destroyed. Whenever you fully destroy a structure, anyone inside will receive damage or could wind up defeated as a result of their injuries.

Supply Drop

Always be on the lookout for Supply Drops. When you discover one landing nearby, approach with caution, and only if you need to expand your arsenal with some potentially powerful and rare weapons.

Instead of approaching a Supply Drop, many experienced players find a good hiding spot near the landing site and wait to ambush enemy soldiers who attempt to reach it. Any long-range weapon, particularly a sniper rifle (or rifle with a scope), or a Rocket Launcher, can be used to launch a surprise attack from a distance.

T

Thermal-Scoped Assault Rifle

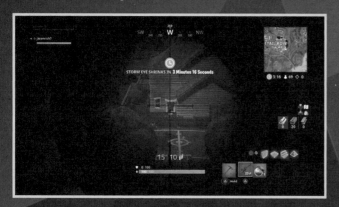

This type of weapon has a scope that allows you to see enemies off in the distance, so you can aim and shoot very precisely. The benefit of a thermal scope is that it allows you to see the heat signatures of enemies hiding inside buildings or fortresses. Shooting at them with a sniper rifle's bullets won't necessarily injure them if they're hiding behind a solid object, but you'll be able to see when they move out into the open, so you can start shooting then.

Tilted Towers

Found at map coordinates D5.5, the first thing you'll notice when you enter Tilted Towers is that it's one of the most popular places on the island, so you're sure to encounter many enemy soldiers here. Be prepared to fight your way through each of the buildings and to continue the firefights on the streets.

If you're planning to land in this area from the Battle Bus, be the first person to wind up on the roof of the clock tower, and then smash your way down toward ground level. Along the way, you'll discover at least three chests by the time you reach ground level.

To easily defeat a few enemies here in Tilted Towers, find a safe position near the top of a building, and then use a shotgun, sniper rifle, or a rifle with a scope to shoot at enemies below. Notice there's an unopened chest in the window in the building across from this soldier. Simply aim your weapon at the chest and wait for an unsuspecting enemy to approach and open it. As soon as you see the enemy in your sights, start shooting.

Each building contains multiple floors and at least several rooms. Don't be surprised if you find enemies hiding. Be extra cautious if you enter a room after hearing footsteps or the sound of a door opening or closing.

If you're brave enough to wander around outside at ground level within Tilted Towers, you'll be rewarded if you're the first to stumble upon the chests, weapons, loot items, and other items lying out in the open. However, watch out for snipers from above, as well as other enemies who are also on ground level. They may be hiding and waiting to ambush any soldier attempting to approach an item, such as this chest.

Because Tilted Towers is such a popular landing spot, you probably won't be the only person landing on a building's roof, if that's where you decide to go. Since you're unarmed when you land, either be the first person to grab a weapon that's lying on the ground or be prepared to do battle using your pickaxe. If you see the roofs of the buildings are crowded, land slightly outside of Tilted Towers, build up your arsenal, and then enter this dangerous area.

Tiptoe

When you have your soldier crouch down and move in any direction, this allows him or her to tiptoe. This is much slower than walking or running, but it makes a lot less noise, especially when indoors. Crouching down also improves your aim when firing any type of weapon.

Tires

Tires can't be collected or smashed for resources, but a soldier can jump on them to gain extra height and use them like a trampoline in order to reach a higher area.

Tomato Temple

Towards the end of Season 5, Tomato Town suddenly changed. Much of what was once in this area was replaced by a giant stone temple that clearly pays homage to Tomatohead. The area is now known as Tomato Temple.

As you explore the temple, you'll discover hidden chambers, in which you'll likely encounter a chest, or at least a few useful items lying on the ground. If you can reach the top of the temple, you'll get a great view of the surrounding area, plus have a height advantage over your adversaries. With the right weapon in hand, you can easily shoot at and defeat enemies below when they try to approach.

Below the stone temple and surrounding it is a large underground area that contains more ancient ruins and places to explore. As you can see, there's a whole network of tunnels and chambers below the house. As you explore this area, there are many places to hide and from which you can launch an ambush on enemies.

Towers

Around the shoreline of the island, you'll discover a bunch of tall watch towers. Each has a different shape. What they all have in common is that they're large. The tower shown here is located near map coordinates B1.

When you encounter one of these towers (this one is on the shoreline, just outside of Wailing Woods near map coordinates J5), either land on the roof after departing from the Battle Bus, climb up the stairs to reach the top, or build a ramp from ground level to reach the top of it.

Traps

Once you pick up one or more Traps, instead of taking up a regular slot within your backpack, an icon for it will appear as part of the Building Mode menu. To later set the Trap, enter into Building mode and select the Trap.

A Trap can be set up on a structure's floor, wall, or ceiling. When an opponent accidently activates the hidden Trap, they'll receive mega-damage. Just make sure you don't set off the Trap yourself once you've activated it, or you'll be the one getting hurt!

Trees

Trees are the greatest source of wood on the island. You'll discover them in smaller quantities within many points of interest. Groups of trees, and even small forests, can be found in the outskirts of many points of interest.

The largest trees can be found in and around Wailing Woods (near map coordinates I3). Your soldier can hide behind or at the top of most trees or use their pickaxe to smash them to harvest wood. When chopping a tree (or any resource for that matter), aim the pickaxe at the target that appears to generate the most units of that resource.

Turbo Building

After turning on this feature from the Settings menu, once you enter into Building mode and choose a building piece and resource type, as long as you hold down the Build trigger button on the controller (or keyboard/mouse) that building piece will keep getting built and placed until you release the Build button or resources run out. Using this feature makes building a ramp or placing walls around you a much faster and easier process.

Twitch Prime Packs

Epic Games has teamed up with Twitch.tv and Amazon.com to periodically offer free, downloadable item packs. To redeem them, you must set up a free Twitch.tv account, and also be a paid Amazon Prime member.

A typical Twitch Prime Pack includes at least one outfit, a matching pickaxe and glider design, several emotes, along with other items for customizing the appearance of your soldier. For more information, visit: www.twitch.tv/prime/fortnite.

U

Unlabeled Points of Interest

In addition to the more than twenty points of interest that are labeled on the map, there are a growing number of locations that are not labeled, but that contain interesting structures, areas, or buildings to explore.

You'll often find unlabeled points of interest along the outer edges (coastline) of the island, and when traveling in between labeled points of interest. The following are just a few of the unlabeled areas you might want to visit during your next match.

Here at map coordinates I5, there's an RV Park that's surrounded by a few structures. You're more apt to find useful items within the structures, but if you navigate your way around the RVs and picnic tables, you'll find weapons, ammo, and loot lying on the ground and on the roofs of some RVs.

There's a container storage depot found near map coordinates H4.5. This one has a bridge overhead that you can walk along in order to get and stay higher than your enemies.

If you check out the area near map coordinates D8, this small area contains a few houses, and a taco restaurant. You'll notice the wooden tower that's shaped like a chair.

Between map coordinates I2.5 and J2.5, right on the coastline of the island (outside of Wailing Woods), you'll discover this house with a massive wooden structure on its roof. If you want to land in a remote spot and quickly gather a ton of weapons, ammo, and loot, this is the perfect spot to begin a match.

Land on top of this structure and smash your way down as you explore. Then make your way inland, avoiding other points of interest during the early stages of a match. You'll be able to stockpile plenty of resources and ammo, while avoiding enemies.

V

Vaulted

When Epic Games removes a weapon, loot item, or something else from the game altogether, the removed item is referred to as having been "vaulted." It could be re-introduced into the game at any time in the future. Jetpacks are an example of a loot item that Epic Games has added and then removed from the game numerous times.

V-Bucks

This is virtual currency used within the game. It can be exchanged for items from the Item Shop, or to purchase a Battle Pass, or unlock a Battle Pass Tier. There are two ways to acquire V-Bucks. You can achieve goals within the game to earn 100 V-Bucks at a time, or you can purchase them (using real money) from the Item Shop.

V-Bucks are sold in bundles of 600 ($4.99 US), 1,000 ($9.99 US), 2,800 ($24.99 US), 7,500 ($59.99 US), or 13,500 ($99.99 US).

Vehicles

Throughout the island, you'll see many abandoned cars, buses, trucks, tractors, ice cream trucks, pickup trucks, RVs, and other vehicles. These can serve several purposes.

Crouch behind vehicles for protection when someone is shooting at you, or when you're shooting at someone else.

Using your pickaxe, smash vehicles (including cars, buses, vans, and trucks) to collect metal. These are one of the best sources of metal on the island. The drawback, however, is that when you start smashing a vehicle, it makes a lot of noise, and will help a nearby enemy determine your location. Often, when you start smashing a car, you'll hear its alarm go off, which makes even more noise.

Vending Machines

Located throughout the island—not just within points of interest—are Vending Machines. Using wood, stone, or metal resources you've collected (not V-Bucks), purchase rare and powerful weapons and loot that are sold from these machines. While the location of the machines is typically consistent from match to match, what's sold within them is not.

Displayed on the front of each Vending Machine are scrolling graphics that show the selection of items available from that machine, as well as each item's price (in resources, not V-Bucks).

To make a purchase, walk directly in front of the Vending Machine and when the item you want is displayed, press the Buy button on your controller (or keyboard/mouse). The item will be dropped in front of you. Pick it up to add it to your Backpack Inventory. However, if your

backpack is already full, you will need to drop an item before acquiring a new one.

Anytime you're standing out in the open, in front of a Vending Machine, watch out for enemy attacks. Consider building walls around you and the Vending Machine for protection, especially if you know multiple enemy soldiers are in the area. If you're not careful, as soon as you make a purchase, an enemy will attack you, eliminate you from the match, and collect your latest purchases (along with everything else you collected during that match).

Viking Village

Located on a mountaintop between map coordinates A5.5 and B5.5 is this Viking village. It's not labeled on the map. The main attraction here is a giant Viking ship.

You can either leap from the Battle Bus and land on top of this mountain, or climb up this dirt path that leads to the mountaintop.

Most of the buildings surrounding the Viking ship contain at least one chest, along with weapons, ammo, loot items, and resource icons lying out in the open. This is a very popular location, so expect to encounter multiple enemies here.

 W

Wailing Woods

At the start of Season 6, the landscape of Wailing Woods was dramatically altered. While this area still contains a lot of trees, in the center of the woods, instead finding a wooden tower, you'll now discover the entrance to a vast underground bunker. Enter into the hedge maze area and work your way toward the center.

When you reach the massive cement block in the center of the hedge maze, find this door and smash it open with your pickaxe, or shoot it a few times until it's demolished.

Jump down and enter into the underground bunker, and then grab whatever loot items or weapons you find when you land.

Once you're in the underground bunker, you'll discover it's massive and contains multiple levels. Start exploring, but proceed with caution, since you may encounter enemy soldiers lurking about.

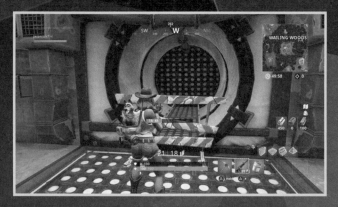

Smash or shoot at barriers in your path in order to travel through tunnels that'll lead you to other areas of the bunker.

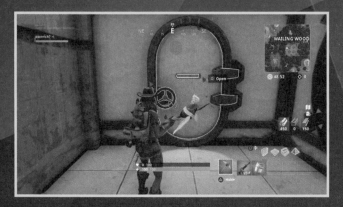

Anytime you approach a solid door and can't see what's on the other side, proceed with caution. If you notice a door has already been opened, chances are there's an enemy nearby. To surprise an enemy, close doors behind you and keep the noise your soldier generates to a minimum.

Some tunnels lead to a dead end. If you hit this type of roadblock, turn around and follow

another route. However, with your back to the cement wall, you can turn around, crouch down, aim your weapon, and then wait for an enemy to pass right in front of you. Since you're in a tunnel, your back and sides will be well protected, so you just have to worry about enemies approaching from the front.

Walk

Walking is one of the ways a soldier moves around the island. Running is faster, while tip-toeing is slower, but makes less noise.

Wall Building Tile

This is one of the four building tile shapes available to you when in Building mode. Wall tiles can be built from wood, stone (shown here), or metal. Depending on what a building tile is made from, this will determine and how much damage it can withstand before collapsing. Face the tile to see its HP meter (in the center of the screen). This stone wall has its full HP strength (300 HP).

Weapon Rarity

Every weapon available in *Fortnite: Battle Royale* has the ability to inflict damage and defeat your adversaries. Some can also easily destroy structures. Each weapon is rated based on several criteria, including its rarity.

Weapons are color-coded with a hue around them to showcase their rarity.

Weapons

There are many types of weapons that you'll discover and can grab on the island. Before engaging in a firefight, however, consider:

- The types of weapons currently in your backpack and available to you.
- The amount of ammo you currently have for each weapon. (Be sure to pick up as much ammo as you can throughout each match.)
- Your distance from an adversary.
- Your surroundings, and whether or not your weapon will need to destroy a barrier, fortress wall, or shielding before it can inflict damage on an enemy.
- Your own skill level as a gamer, and your speed when it comes to selecting, targeting/aiming, and then firing your weapon.

In each weapon category, up to a dozen or more different types of weapons may become accessible to you. Epic Games regularly tweaks the selection of weapons available, as well as the capabilities of each weapon.

Western Town

Located in the desert region, near map coordinates H9.5, is this Western town. It contains a cluster of buildings and structures, almost all of which contain a chest, or at least a few weapons, ammo, loot items, and resource icons lying out in the open.

This is a great place to land after departing the Battle Bus. You can quickly build up your arsenal, while encountering few enemies. You're then free to travel to Paradise Palms, Lucky Landing, or any other area of the island.

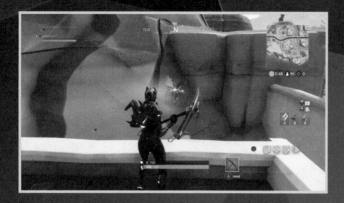

Wood

Wood is one of the three resources you'll need to collect during a match. When it comes to building, wood is the fastest resource to work with. It's great for quickly constructing ramps, or for creating small forts that'll offer basic protection if attacked. Both stone and metal are stronger materials that better resist incoming attacks, but they're slower to build with.

You'll likely discover Rifts in this area, which you can use to travel to other parts of the island quickly. Sometimes, you'll also come across a parked ATK that you can drive out of the area.

Wood pallets that are scattered throughout the island (and found within many points of interest) provide a great source of wood. Smash wood pallets with your pickaxe.

SECTION 4

FORTNITE: BATTLE ROYALE RESOURCES

On YouTube (www.youtube.com) or Twitch. TV (www.twitch.tv/directory/game/Fortnite), in the Search field, enter the search phrase "*Fortnite: Battle Royale*" to discover many game-related channels, livestreams, and prerecorded videos that'll help you become a better player.

Also, be sure to check out these other online resources:

WEBSITE OR YOUTUBE CHANNEL NAME	DESCRIPTION	URL
Fandom's *Fortnite* Wiki	Discover the latest news and strategies related to *Fortnite: Battle Royale*.	http://fortnite.wikia.com/wiki/Fortnite_Wiki
FantasticalGamer	A popular YouTuber who publishes *Fortnite* tutorial videos.	www.youtube.com/user/FantasticalGamer
FBR Insider	The *Fortnite: Battle Royale Insider* website offers game-related news, tips, and strategy videos.	www.fortniteinsider.com
Fortnite Gamepedia Wiki	Read up-to-date descriptions of every weapon, loot item, and ammo type available within *Fortnite: Battle Royale.* This Wiki also maintains a comprehensive database of soldier outfits and related items released by Epic Games.	https://fortnite.gamepedia.com/Fortnite_Wiki
Fortnite Intel	An independent source of news related to *Fortnite: Battle Royale*.	www.fortniteintel.com
Fortnite Scout	Check your personal player stats, and analyze your performance using a bunch of colorful graphs and charts. Also check out the stats of other *Fortnite: Battle Royale* players.	www.fortnitescout.com
Fortnite Stats & Leaderboard	This is an independent website that allows you to view your own *Fortnite*-related stats or discover the stats from the best players in the world.	https://fortnitestats.com
Game Informer Magazine's *Fortnite* Coverage	Discover articles, reviews, and news about *Fortnite: Battle Royale* published by *Game Informer* magazine.	www.gameinformer.com/search/searchresults.aspx?q=Fortnite
GameSpot's *Fortnite* Coverage	Check out the news, reviews, and game coverage related to *Fortnite: Battle Royale* that's been published by GameSpot.	www.gamespot.com/fortnite

(continued on next page)

IGN Entertainment's *Fortnite* Coverage	Check out all IGN's past and current coverage of *Fortnite*.	www.ign.com/wikis/fortnite
Jason R. Rich's Website and Social Media Feeds	Share your *Fortnite: Battle Royale* game play strategies with this book's author and learn about his other books.	www.JasonRich.com www.FortniteGameBooks.com Twitter: @JasonRich7 Instagram: @JasonRich7
Microsoft's Xbox One *Fortnite* Website	Learn about and acquire *Fortnite: Battle Royale* if you're an Xbox One gamer.	https://www.microsoft.com/en-us/p/fortnite-battle-royale/bt5p2x999vh2
MonsterDface YouTube and Twitch.tv Channels	Watch video tutorials and live game streams from an expert *Fortnite* player.	www.youtube.com/user/MonsterdfaceLive www.Twitch.tv/MonsterDface
Ninja	Check out the live and recorded game streams from Ninja, one of the most highly skilled *Fortnite: Battle Royale* players in the world on Twitch.tv and YouTube.	www.twitch.tv/ninja_fortnite_hyper www.youtube.com/user/NinjasHyper
Official Epic Games YouTube Channel for *Fortnite: Battle Royale*	The official *Fortnite: Battle Royale* YouTube channel.	www.youtube.com/user/epicfortnite
Turtle Beach Corp.	This is one of many companies that make great quality, wired or wireless (Bluetooth) gaming headsets that work with all gaming platforms.	www.turtlebeach.com

Your *Fortnite: Battle Royale* Adventure Continues . . .

With more than 125 million active players, in just over one year, *Fortnite: Battle Royale* has become one of the most popular games in the world. After reading this unofficial strategy guide, you now have the basic knowledge needed to begin playing this action-packed and exciting game.

Just remember, to become really good at playing *Fortnite: Battle Royale* takes a lot of practice! Don't allow yourself to get frustrated early on, especially if you keep getting quickly defeated during matches. Learn from your mistakes, and each time you visit the island for a new match, try to remember what you discovered at various island locations, and use that knowledge to your advantage to help you quickly build up your arsenal and stockpile ammo.

Fortnite: Battle Royale requires players to master the art of safely exploring the island, building, fighting, and avoiding the storm. You'll need to discover which loot items and weapons to use in order to achieve the desired results, based on the situations you encounter at any given moment. Be ready to alter your strategy, based on the actions of your enemy, and always try to benefit by using the terrain that surrounds you.

Remember, you'll almost always have a tactical advantage if you're higher up than your enemies, especially during an intense firefight. As you begin playing *Fortnite: Battle Royale*, consider spending time in the Playground game play mode if it's available. This will help you get better acquainted with the island and all of the weapons, loot items, ammo types, and resources that are at your disposal.

Finally, regardless of which game play mode you experience, always plan on having fun while playing *Fortnite: Battle Royale*. The more you play, the better you'll become!